Diva
FIVE ALIVE

letters to my Sisters

DR. JULIE ANN GRAY
MARILYN MCBRIDE, BRENDA J. MILLER
CAROLYN GIBERT, EVETTE GIBERT

Diva Five Alive
Letters to My Sisters

Copyright © 2018 by Dr. Julie Ann Gray

All rights reserved. No part of this book may be reproduced or transmitted in any form or by any means without written permission of the author.

In order to respect privacy, the names of many of the people mentioned (other than the authors) have been changed.

Edited by: Laurel Ornitz
Cover by: 99designs

ISBN 978-1-7326570-0-7 (paperback)
ISBN 978-1-7326570-1-4 (eBook)

Published by:
Church Street Publishing House

Dedication

*This book is dedicated to the memory of our mother,
Bernadine Elizabeth McBride Gibert, the original Diva,
whose spirit is still alive and continues to inspire us to never give up!*

Contents

Introduction 1
1 Bernadine: What's in a Name? 9
2 Let's Get This Letter-Writing Party Started:
   Our First Sister Letters 19
3 I Wonder What She Wished For 29
4 Hero Child.. 35
5 Relationships 49
6 Church and Holiday Memories......................... 61
7 Scary and Dangerous Times 79
8 Fun Times 93
9 Mental Illness... 101
10 Big Lind 107
11 Lil Lind 113
12 Wrapping It Up 121
About the Contributors..................................... 129
Acknowledgements 133

Introduction

"Then the Lord replied: 'Write down the revelation and make it plain on tablets so that a herald may run with it. For the revelation awaits an appointed time; it speaks of the end and will not prove false. Though it lingers, wait for it: it will certainly come and will not delay.'"

—Habakkuk 2:2–4

FEBRUARY 25, 2014

Starting this project, I thought, I am not going to let another dream or idea die. As hard as it is sometimes, I continue to pick up the pieces of what I sometimes consider my shattered life and dreams. In the same vein, I am picking up the pieces of this project. I have literally gotten up out of my chair (which is a huge feat for me these days) and plugged up my printer with the intent of organizing and printing all the "sister letters" I have collected to date. This idea did not just fall out of the sky, as earlier today, I found out about a resource by which people can self-publish a book.

I have decided to pick up where I started and that is with my mother, Bernadine Elizabeth McBride Gibert. I include her maiden name because the legacy of her maiden name was a great part of who she was. I thought about how when it finally registered that she was really going to die from pancreatic cancer and it was just a matter of time—time she didn't have enough energy to squeeze into traveling on a plane, which she had never done, or going to a circus, as she longed to do—how I should not let time continue to get away from me.

JANUARY 13, 2013

> *"They overcame him by the blood of the Lamb and by the word of their testimony."*
> —Revelation 12:11

I was reading *Essence* magazine today and ran across an article written by Iyanla Vanzant, an inspirational speaker, author, life coach, and television personality. In the article, she gave ten steps to claiming your joy. One step is to testify. "I try to be as transparent as possible, because people lied to me all my life. It's important that we share our experiences with other people," she said. "Your story will heal you and your story will heal somebody else. As you put your truth out there, you allow other people to experience life from a different perspective. When you tell your story, you free yourself and give other people permission to acknowledge their own story." This statement really resonated with me, as I believe there is a lot of power in sharing, and you never know who you might encourage.

Another quote that has a lot of meaning for me is this one by Howard Thurman. Howard Thurman is a philosopher, theologian, educator, author, and civil rights leader. "The dreams belong to us; they come full-blown out of the real world in which we work and hope and carry on. They are not impostors. They are not foreign elements invading our world like some solitary comet from the outer reaches of space which pays one visit to the sun and is going to never come again. No! Our dreams are our thing. They become other when we let them lose their character. Here is the fatal blunder: our dreams must be saddled by the hard facts of our world before we ride them off amongst the stars. Thus, they become for us the bearers of the new possibility, the enlarged horizon, the great hope. Even as they romp among the stars, they come back to their place in our lives, bringing with them the radiance of the far heights, the lofty regions, and giving to all our days the lift and the magic of the stars." This quote reminds me of my dreams and especially my dreams for this book, and even though I have delayed and put it off several times, it continues to come back to its place in my life.

DECEMBER 2, 2014

Brenda (Little Diva) created a drawing titled "Diva, 5 Alive" and sent it to us after a prayer call, and I thought, wow, that's the name of our book! As I sit here today, December 2, 2014, writing the introduction to this story about five very much alive sisters by blood and experience, I find myself thinking about how the word *Diva* came about for us.

It was Marilyn who coined the term (though not the original person to coin it) and with that honor comes the honor of calling her "Big Diva." With that said, since you can only have one "Big Diva" in a family of sisters, Brenda, who is next in line by age, became "Lil Diva." Carolyn was coined "Diva in the Making," as she is next in line by age. Now me... I am not sure if an official Diva name was ever decided for me, and I will get to the reasons I believe so in a minute. Evette, the youngest sister, is the Lilest Diva. Being a Diva means being sharp, classy, and sassy. It means knowing how to dress to impress. It means keeping that hair and those nails done, loving to shop, and having lots of nice clothes, shoes, and purses to show for it.

I guess that is why I was never given a Diva name, as no one could figure out what to call me. I've never really had a good fashion sense. I hate shopping, and I never conformed to what was considered a Diva, such as having straight hair and lots of clothes, purses, etc. My sisters laugh at me because I usually only own one tube of lipstick, normally only change my purse during the change of seasons, and was the first of my sisters to go "natural" with my hair.

I remember when I had my hair chopped off to get rid of the perm and was wearing twists, natural pony tails, braids, or whatever I could get my natural hair to do, until I decided to let it lock into dreadlocks. At one point, Marilyn asked Brenda, "What's up with Julie's hair?" She just couldn't figure out why I was not a Diva like the rest of them! LOL!

Being the thinker I am, I also thought about why Brenda did not make the word *Diva* plural. I remember making a mental note to myself to ask her to re-do the title of the drawing adding a "s" to the end of the word *Diva*. Then it dawned on me, yes there are five of us sisters who share the same DNA, but we are each so unique, just as God made us. With that said, Diva, in lieu of Divas, signifies individuality or singular experiences involving the whole of us. So yes, we are Diva Five, Alive!

Of course, I am not done overanalyzing, even though at the end of the day, I know that the plan to bring forth this book was inspired by and came into being through God. But I can't help

Introduction

think about when we will not be "Diva Five, Alive" in the body, and I wanted to be sure that this wasn't just another God-inspired project that I put aside. I want our story to be shared while we are still alive. I am hoping the miracle of all of us still being alive becomes apparent as you read our book. We hope that it will inspire you to continue on your journey, realizing that with God all things are possible! So here is some of our story told to you in a collection of letters and other ways. We hope and pray that you will be inspired to understand your own aliveness through this, as well.

With love,
Jewels

JUNE 11, 2017

Picking up the project again, we are the five living daughters of Bernadine Elizabeth McBride Gibert. Our names are Marilyn Elizabeth McBride (Big Diva), Brenda Jean Gibert-Miller (Lil Diva), Carolyn Ruth Gibert (Diva in the making/Sadie/Granny), Julie Ann Gibert Gray (me/Jewels), and Evette Marie Gibert. The sixth daughter died in my mother's womb as the result of one of many beatings she suffered at the hands of my father. At the time of this writing, our ages are sixty-four, sixty-three, sixty-two, fifty-nine, and fifty-seven. Marilyn is a retired social service worker who has been living with HIV for twenty-five plus years. She is also the manager of the senior apartment building in which she lives. Brenda is the senior pastor of a small rural church who has been living sober from alcohol and drugs for over twenty-eight years. Carolyn is an educator who is living with multiple health challenges as a result of sickle cell disease and has also been drug free

Diva Five Alive

for years. Julie is a psychologist and a licensed clinical social worker in private practice who is living with major depressive disorder and has been free from a cocaine addiction for over twenty-nine years. Evette is a crew trainer with a major fast food chain who continues to struggle to maintain sobriety from substance abuse.

As this book will reveal, our memories of our childhood differ, but we are all still the children of Bernadine Elizabeth McBride Gibert. Even though this book is primarily a sharing of sister letters and our stories, I need to mention that we have brothers, too. They are Lindbergh Gibert (deceased), Floyd Gibert, Michael Allan Gibert, and Kevin Lamont Gibert. It is also rumored that we have other brothers whom our father fathered by the same woman who is the mother of our stepsister, Lynn, but never acknowledged as being his sons. Lynn did not grow up with us, thus the reason for her not being included in the sister letters.

The idea for this book came about in January of 2012 when Brenda mentioned that she wanted to write a book about a recently deceased pastor/mentor friend of hers. I then said we should write a book using letters we had written to each other over the years. I had the idea of exchanging sister letters when I began to realize through our conversations that our memories of childhood events were usually different or not remembered at all. The concept I came up with was that the eldest sister would start by writing a letter about any memory she had of her childhood, or any thought that came to mind. The other sisters would write a response, and then we would rotate, with the next-eldest sister starting the letter chain.

Let me continue the introduction of our book with introducing you further to our mother, Bernie. Bernadine Elizabeth McBride Gibert was the youngest of four sisters born to Sally McBride and Clifton McBride on September 25, 1936, in Evanston, Illinois. There is some controversy over her birth, as her birth certificate

Introduction

has the date of her birth as some date in October. However, as told to us, her mother said she "knows the day" her daughter was born and insists that it was September 25, 1936, so that is the date we have always acknowledged and celebrated as her birthday. (I also need to add that my eldest daughter, Nicole shares Bernie's birthday.) Who knows what hospitals did back then, especially at Community Hospital, which was the only hospital for blacks at that time. Blacks weren't allowed at Evanston Hospital. Bernie, as she was affectionately known and called, even by her children, also had four brothers, making a total of nine children born into the McBride family.

In April of 1955, Bernie married Lindberg Gibert, and from that union, eight children were born. Marilyn was born out of wedlock to a different father when Bernie was sixteen years old. However, the word *stepsister* never applied when we thought of Marilyn. However, it did apply when we thought of Lynn, a daughter born to my father and a woman he was seeing at the same time he was seeing my mother. Lynn was born a few months before Brenda was born.

This book is an account of our memories, victories, struggles, testimonies, hurts, pains, learning lessons, and more. We hope it blesses you as it blessed us as we wrote each "sister letter."

Bernie

CHAPTER 1
Bernadine: What's in a Name?

"You can call me whatever you want. Just don't call me late to dinner!"
—Bernadine Elizabeth McBride Gibert

"A good name is more desirable than great riches; to be esteemed is better than silver or gold."
—Proverbs 22:1

DECEMBER 2012

Divas,

Growing up, all I wanted was a mother. I found Bernie was easy to talk to, easy to get along with, etc., until she changed, or life changed her, but she was always our mother regardless.

I remember one time she hosed a neighborhood boy down with the garden hose. She wet him up and stuck the water hose in his pants. He must have done something disrespectful to her. I remember how he screamed and ran home, and Bernie chased him until he reached his front porch, and when his mother opened the door, Bernie told her what happened. I remember at that point I didn't think he would ever come in our backyard and play around with our mother or play with us again.

I also remember how I would get mad, not jealous, but mad, especially at my boyfriend and some of my girlfriends, for having such a casual relationship with our mother. All I wanted was for other people to call our mother Ms. Gibert or show her some sign of respect.

It dawned on me that we referred to her as Bernie, and I don't ever remember calling her Mother or Bernadine, just referring to her as Bernie when speaking to my siblings, whatever the situation, or listening to my friends and acquaintances referring to her as Bernie. When speaking to Bernie myself, my sentences always started off with "Can you...," "How do you...," "How are you...," "Can I...," or something like that. I guess it felt awkward as a kid not calling our mother Mother or Mama, but I don't really remember giving her a title. I thought, Well, we don't call her Mother or Mama or Mom because she did not want us to, or did not train us to do so.

I remember her befriending Bernie, the man at Centrella's grocery store, where we could go and get her cigarettes or whatever till payday. She would joke sometimes and say it was a man's name, too, but I never really knew what she felt about us calling her anything other than Bernie.

I remember Little Lind referred to her as Momma all the time, whether he was sick or well. When we shared bedrooms, I remember him calling for her. He was the only one of us who called her Momma.

I also remember our father making us call her names and say cuss words to her. I felt so bad, and I was scared looking up at her,

Bernadine: What's in a Name?

and more afraid if I did not repeat what Big Lind would tell me to say to her. I wondered, if she didn't want us to call her Mother, if he didn't want us to call her Mother, or if we were conditioned not to call her Mother because we called Grandma Sally, Mama and possibly heard our mother and her siblings call her mother Mama as well.

I felt awkward when my friends called their mother Mother or when I went over to someone's house and referred to their parents by Mr., Mrs., or Ms., and not by their first name.

That's what I remember and how it affected me. Now that I'm not a kid and have a grown daughter of my own, I think it is disrespectful. I couldn't imagine my daughter calling me by my first name.

Straight from the heart,
Sadie

Divas,

Somewhere in my mind, I hear Momma (Grandmother Sally McBride) saying, "Bernadine!" I don't know if that is a childhood memory of me hearing my mother called or was it just the way Momma could say Bernadine, with such force and seriousness! I never heard her call her daughter Bernie.

For me, the first directive I recall on what to call my mother was her saying "Don't call me Momma. I don't want anybody thinking I am old enough to have all these kids." Perhaps this should not be in quotes, because it may not be absolutely correct, but it is close enough.

I can see her saying it, dressed in Bermuda stretch shorts and a sleeveless shell, breasts held high up with a good bra, hand on hip, cigarette in red nail-polished hand, going to her red lips, all the while breaking out in that beautiful smile.

She was sort of joking, but not really. As I recall, that meant "Shoot, I am still young enough and fine enough. I sure don't look like a woman who could have so many children."

And that was all good it seemed, and innocent enough, but latter years brought problems, as Bernie seemed to not grow up into her adult mother responsibilities, or better put, I would say she reverted back to her younger years, once our father died and she really thought she was one of us.

When I was a child, I thought it was cool to call her Bernie and other kids did too. Once I explained that we could call her that because she wanted us to, they were like "Wow, my mother would knock my head off if I called her by her name. You sure got a cool mother."

I felt that our friends calling her Bernie was in no way disrespectful. In fact, I think many of my friends felt like she was more of a mother to them than their own mothers, which seems strange because often my own maternal needs were not met.

But again, as I got older, it was not so cool, as I did not want my mother trying to hang out with my friends and me and be one of us, and she did that all the time. It used to make me mad and sometimes I felt embarrassed.

This letter could go on and on, but this is my stopping point. I remember the eulogy that Pastor Curry preached for our "mom" (something I had started to call her more often once I got sober); it was titled "The God That Bernie Knew."

The point the eulogy made was that so many people knew and loved Bernie just the way she was and she loved everybody she met. She was just "Bernie" to everybody. She introduced herself that way, did not put on any airs or pretense about being somebody she was not, and didn't care if you knew her business.

Bernadine: What's in a Name?

She was just herself, whether you liked how she presented herself or not. And who didn't like Bernie?

In summary, Pastor Curry said, "As different and peculiar as Bernie was, she was loving and lovable and she knew her God, who loved her just as she was." I am paraphrasing this as well as I can remember.

That's Bernie, Bernadine Elizabeth McBride-Gibert, a strong woman, who knew and loved her God, and who now, today, I realize, I was blessed to have as my mother.

Peace and Love,
Lil Diva

Divas,

In response to Granny's "What's in a Name?" letter and my cheating reading Brenda's before I responded, I found I had the same sentiments as Brenda, that I would be mad at Bernie for hanging out with my friends, getting high with us, etc. I would also be embarrassed. I remember hanging around my friend, Barbara, and wishing that Bernie could be like her mother, all proper and prissy and being called Mom.

I remember when Bernie was thirty-six (I don't know why that age sticks out, but it does. Thinking back then, I thought that was so old!). Anyway, I remember thinking how she was too old to be wearing "sizzle suits" and going to the Lion's Den, and that she should have been staying home taking care of her kids.

I do believe that Bernie was trying to recapture her youth, which was lost because of an early marriage and having so many kids at such a young age. Knowing my struggles of raising four, I can't imagine how she did it. I remember thinking that when my youngest children, Naomi and Joshua, were both in diapers at the same time, how that was the hardest thing I had ever done in my life, raising these young children so close in age. Bernie not only had kids in diapers at the same time, but also hanging onto her breasts, running around the house, being sick, etc. I think she was twenty-one when she had me and I was her fifth child! Wow, a fifth child at age twenty-one! What a life!

I do remember one other special name Bernie was called: Sis. Her favorite brother Edward would call her that whenever he would come to visit and that was almost every day after he finished his work as a "garbage man" for the City of Evanston.

I remember one particular time he was there and I had just gotten my period for the first time. Bernie told him to go to the store and buy some Kotex for me. He said, "Shit, put a piece of newspaper on her ass." I remember being so embarrassed as a young twelve-year-old, because, first of all, he knew I started my period, and, secondly, by his comment. Bernie just laughed and told him, "Boy, go to the store and get her some Kotex," which he promptly did.

I also remember how he would mix up concoctions, such as raw eggs, hot sauce, etc., and drink it. I think those were his remedies for getting rid of hangovers. I also remember how devastated Bernie was when he died. I called her on the day, as I was no longer living at home, just to say hi, I think. She sounded really sad, and I asked her what was wrong, and she said, "Edward had a heart attack." I asked her if he was okay, and she said, "No, he died." On that day, Bernie lost her brother, who brought her so much joy and laughter and called her Sis.

Anyway, in the words of our pastor, "Bernie was loving and loved by many." She often sacrificed her happiness to make others happy and many people used her and took her kindness for a weakness. Bernie would say, "Call me whatever you want, but just don't call me late for dinner" and "See ya later alligator, after while crocodile." I thought that was funny. I remember thinking at her eulogy "Bernie, Mom, we will all see you again. I already miss you!"

With love,
Jewels

Hey Divas,

I remember so clearly Mama saying, "Why do you all call your mother Bernie?" I never knew why—I just did because you all did, I guess. I thought Mama was my mother for a long time in my younger days when I was unable to understand who was who, but because Mama did all the things my mother was supposed to do. It was weird.

All I know is I loved Bernie, whatever she was called, for what's in a name? All I know is she was a great mom. I remember when she would press our hair and how I would stare at her whenever I had to face her when getting my bangs done. I would kiss her real fast and hug her waist so hard. I remember how that sweat would be on her nose and how she would look surprised sometimes when I hugged her. She was lovely, beautiful, smelled so nice, and that smile would knock you out. I do remember everyone saying, "You call your mother by her first name?" But that seemed cool. I would never have said "Sally" to Mama (laugh), but she was not Mama, she was Bernie, which so fit her, so really, what's in a name? I struggled just to know her, so it did not bother me one bit what she was called. That was my mother.

I think Mama used to get nervous when I would come to visit or be gone for the weekend. She often looked sad, as if I was not coming back, and I would talk on and on, saying, "Bernie did this and Bernie said that," when I would come home, and Momma would just look and smile. She knew how much I wanted to be with Bernie and you guys, too.

I was lucky to have "Bernie" as a mother because everyone loved her. I just wish that she would have gotten to really know how sad it made me, how often I thought of her. Like now with my grand- and great-grandchildren being born, makes you think. So really, names are overrated, because some who are called Mother, Mama, or whatever, did not compare to ours. Her compassion for people and love for us, as far as I'm concerned, that was her name.

So there you have it,
Big Diva

Divas,

Well, in reading everyone's letters, I can truly relate to them and could validate mostly everything that was said, especially the things Julie said. I remember Julie telling me the story about Bernie sending Uncle Edward to get Kotex for her. I do remember him and Uncle Richard coming over to the house, but I don't remember a whole lot more.

I can remember having feelings like Bernie did not care about us and being mad because she would not make Julie get up and go to school with me, or not even caring if I went.

I wasn't expecting Bernie to show up at my graduation, but I remember being so happy when I looked out in the audience and saw her there. I can't really say what I felt when my friends would come over to the house before parties and get pills or whatever to get high off from Bernie.

Bernadine: What's in a Name?

I could go on and on writing about Bernie (Mom), but all I know is I watched her go through so much hurt and pain in life, and I know she truly loved us all the best she could after everything she went through in life. Having feeling like not being such a good mother to my children and having a son who doesn't call me Mom or Evette, this was a topic I really needed to touch base on.

It also brought closure and understanding to the haunting feelings I have been carrying with me for years of not showing up at Bernie's funeral.

With all that being said, I just want to say Bernie (Mom) I love and miss you so much. The last time I saw your face, I remember you saying to me, "You're saying bye to me now." Now I know why you said to me, "See you later alligator, after while crocodile," and I can feel you laughing.

I love you Mom!

Love,
Ms. Evette

Bernie and Julie

CHAPTER 2

Let's Get This Letter-Writing Party Started: Our First Sister Letters

"For God has not given us the spirit of fear, but of power and of love and of a sound mind."

—2 Timothy 1:7

JANUARY 2013

Hey Divas,

Well, we are into 2013, and I am excited! I'm feeling good, and I plan to catch up on some things that I have put off doing, and cleaning up my office is a start!

I was glad to see Little Diva and Ken. The service Friday was awesome—so many great memories and so many people loved Rev. Little. That is a great legacy. I know her children were blown away by the outpouring of love and spirit there. So that gives me fuel to carry on. We have much work to do. I put things off, I complain, I doubt, but I really should be grateful for the legacy of Rev. Little the Lord placed in me. We all have degrees of greatness, and what we do with it, well, that's a different story—your story, our story.

I have just one more thing to add. I am coming out of this fear this year! The thought, I am not good enough—how insane is that? How great are the gifts God has given us. Do we use them all? No, we don't because we are not aware of them, we don't know what they are.

Speaking for myself, I need to really (this year) seek God. I mean really seek Him! I must stop playing church, stop looking at others, and keep my eyes on Him, and find out who I really am! I hope this all makes sense, all this venting. Love you guys.

So there you have it,
Big Diva

Hey Big Diva,

Your letter was so on target, right out of my heart, right in my message for yesterday, and always the message comes to the messenger first. So my check for if my sermon is truly a word from God, is, does it apply to my life? And the answer is yes, it does, each and every one of them in some way.

I have felt in 2012 as though I was losing my momentum and my passion, and it was due to looking at all that was wrong, instead of what was right. And right is God and being focused on keeping my relationship with Him first, which means before preaching, teaching, counseling, putting out fires, begging people to come out

Let's Get This Letter-Writing Party Started: Our First Sister Letters

of the dark who want to stay there, wanting folks to be sober more than they want to be, crying inside because folks are loose living and God desires for us to be sanctified vessels fit for His use, before preaching my head off, as you said "screaming" (and I don't care), and watching the Spirit fall like fire, and once the benediction is announced, oh well, for many, not all, I did church! So, let's get to hometown or whatever it is we are going to do! I can see folk gossiping and clicking, and they have not even got out of the door.

But yesterday before I preached, Chelle played, "I Will Put On My Robe and Tell My Story How I Made It Over." And I thought, my goodness, I am going to pass out and start crying and not be able to preach. Why is she playing that song? I wondered, but the exact opposite happened! I felt a peace, I felt myself moving forward in my grief, I saw Rev. B. in my spirit's eye with one of her best robes on smiling and saying, "I made it over." Once the song was over and voices left the pulpit, Chelle played, "Thank You Lord," which was the same song they played at the end of the eulogy Saturday. I mouthed, "Thank you," to her, and she smiled this very peculiar smile, and I knew although she is keenly connected to my spirit, that God was using her in an unusual way. So, I stood like my mentor and preached like there was no tomorrow. As someone said about her in the service, and as I said what God said, "Yes and amen."

The revelation of Revelations 21 and 22 is that this book is not about the end of the world, but about the beginning. After the seven plagues, the calamities and curses that destroyed the earth, John saw a new heaven and a new earth coming down from the throne of God. He saw the city of Jerusalem all adorned with gems and the pearly gates and streets of gold, and then he saw the pure river of the water of life and there was the tree of life that bore twelve fruits—fruit for each month of the year.

And so, as I end preaching the mini sermon to myself and my sisters again, God said He promised to restore, remake, rebuild, and make us better, no matter what the devastation, destruction, plague, or whatever, but the expectation of us is that we bear fruit, as each month's end ought to find us closer to God, tighter with Him, and more healed and less wounded.

We think 2012 went by fast! Watch 2013—it is going to go even quicker, and that is because Jesus is coming back soon. He said it three times in Revelation 22, and I want to be ready. I want the reward He is going to give for our works. I don't want to be left outside the gate! I want to live each day like it was my last, fighting till the end, if I have to, like Rev. B., because she got her crown, and I intend to get mine! So, I am fueled, re-energized. I don't care if the marriage ain't right, if the church folk don't act right. I don't care what anything negative looks like because I am walking by faith and not by sight. I am not gonna whine and complain (and I do); I will not give the devil the pleasure of thinking he has me bound. I am going to vision it and write it and watch God work it and make it come to pass!

As if this day was my last, when I close my eyes, I want to have accomplished what God intended for me to do. Like someone said at the Saturday service regarding Rev. B., "Dying is holy business." So she was about God's business, even till the end!

I know this is not the right subject for the letters to my sisters, but I needed to say it, and I thank the Lord I have sisters who will take the time to read it when they can.

Peace and Love,
Lil Diva

Let's Get This Letter-Writing Party Started: Our First Sister Letters

Hey Divas,

Happy New Year! Now I am not one to make New Year's resolutions, but I want to stay excited about what this year will bring for me, for you, and for us. Like Big Diva said, we all have degrees of greatness, and even though our stories are different, they are indeed your stories, our stories.

Sometimes, no, many times, I get comfortable with mediocrity, and most of the time, I am so tired that I just want to go to work and come home and relax. Not that I shouldn't relax, but God has much bigger plans for my life, your lives. I am often reminded of having to follow the dictates of people at work who don't know the bottom from the top. Not that I don't respect authority, because I do, but I know that is God's way of telling me it is time to be the head and not the tail. What holds me back? Fear, yes, laziness, yes, feeling I am not good enough, yes, all of those things. No, it is not insane, Big Diva, it is what it is. But you know what, many great people, past and present, have felt the same way, but have pushed through to greatness. Why can't I? Why can't you? Why can't we?

Sometimes I think about the root of feelings of inadequacy. Did they come from a mother who told me that I would "never grow up to be shit" or from a father who snuck in my bed at night, leaving me with the message that if a man wants to have sex, that equates to love? How stupid is that?

Anyway, I am beginning to ramble now. Perhaps my flu virus is kicking back in. But whatever the cause of my rambling, my fears, doubts, and insecurities, though present, are not really relevant. I will begin to say to myself that I am more than a conqueror and that "I can do all things through Christ, who strengthens me" (Philippians 4:13) and who will withhold no good thing from me.

Love,
Jewels

Divas,

I believe that fear isn't intentionally taught to us, but it's learned through life experiences, situations, and circumstances. Think of the innocence a child is born with and maintains until he or she discovers fear through people, places, or things, which negates life experiences, situations, and circumstances. Sometimes the little person in us all wants to maintain a sense of innocence. We desire to go back to that place where nothing matters, nothing hurts, and nothing causes us fear. Well, we all would have to go back to the childhood years of innocence before we were tainted by life experiences, situations, and circumstances.

What keeps us in fear is not the person, place, or thing that causes the fear or our unforgiving spirit, but the inability to wash the memory of fear from our minds. It's in our mental capacity where we control our thoughts and emotions. Even our ability to breathe in and exhale is controlled by the mind. We all know the feeling of fear, that emotion when we breathe and our heart patters, as fear knocks at the door of our hearts. I'm here to tell you, if you do not let fear enter your heart, it will eventually leave your mind alone. Proverbs 4:23 says, "Keep your heart with all diligence, for out of it are the issues of life."

The heart is the place where emotions are felt; it controls our will to be or not to be. The heart has the ability to determine our joy and fears; it determines whether we are going to feel happy or sad. The enemy tries to control our minds, but we have the ability and the God-given authority to guard our hearts. Therefore, if we are unable to control the source of our fear, we are incapable of fully living up to our God-given potential.

Okay, you may read this and think, this sister has it all together. She's not like me; she has forgotten all of her fears. No, I say, I have not forgotten. In fact, I remember when the fear of success first showed its ugly face to me. I was a child, and my mother hindered me with her "learned" fears. She told me, along with the doctors, that I could not ride a bike, that I could not do what other children did. Even as I reached adulthood, she, along with the doctors, told me I could not keep my baby! And, oh, as if that were not enough, perhaps my fear of financial gain comes from my father's fears and his inability to trust me or others. He beat me for babysitting and making money, huh? Perhaps these are reasons enough for the enemy to see an opening to lead me down a dangerous path of destruction years ago. But thank God as He is the Great Deliverer!

I declare that the Lord has given us authority over those childhood fears. As 2 Timothy 1:7 says, "For God has not given us a spirit of fear, but of power and of love and of a sound mind." And I declare on this day, at this moment, that the enemy has no place where the power of God resides. Speak it into your spirit until that uneasy feeling that's knocking at the door of your heart leaves. Because remember, your heart is guarded and you have the authority not to let evil enter into it. God is so good, even comanding his angels to guard us. As Psalm 91:11 says, "God gives His Angels charge of [us] to guard [us] in all of [our] ways."

Prayer: Lord, in the name of Jesus, I pray to you right now that the memory of my fears will cease to have authority over my mind and my thoughts. You have already given me the Godly authority not to let fear enter into my heart, and I declare I will exercise that authority. I pray for easement and clarity today, oh Lord. I pray that the power of Your Holy Spirit, which lives in me, would be greater than the emotion of fear. I demand by the power of the Holy Spirit and through the name of Jesus, our intercessor, that fear leave and abide in me no more. I claim in the name of Jesus the Christ that fear has no authority where the power of God resides, and that power and authority over my emotions, especially fear, resides in me today, and forevermore, in Jesus' name and for His sake, Amen! For it's through life's experiences, situations, and circumstances that we all have choices to make.

I thank God for being the middle sister, as I get to evolve from both ends of the sister spectrum. I thank you, Big Diva, for the mention of fear, for that mere mention brings healing. I thank you, Lil Diva, for listening to God's calling. And I thank you, Jewels, for your openness and honesty.

Straight from the heart,
Sadie

Hey Divas, my beautiful sisters,

I must admit when I first heard about this letter-writing idea, something in my head said, "Oh no, I don't want to do this." I have been writing letters for eighteen months to a certain individual and I don't like doing it mainly because half the stuff I am saying is not the truth, but then something clicked. The message was, write from your heart. It said nothing about what's in your head. It might sound strange, but I do separate the two. Sometimes the things that are going on in my head are not what I feel in my heart, but the thoughts in my head seem to overpower my heart, and that's not good. Yes, indeed, I can relate to a lot of the things my big sister said in her letter, such as not being good enough, find out who I really am, and to seek God, and not be afraid of the outcome. I truly pray that this year I can let go and just let God so I can be set free. There is so much more to be revealed, so until the next time.

Love,
Ms. Evette

Bernie

CHAPTER 3

I Wonder What She Wished For

"Ask whatever you wish and it will be given you."
—John 15:7

NOVEMBER 2014

"Come on Julie," Maria said in her thick Portuguese accent, "break this with me." I looked and she was extending to me the wishbone from the Thanksgiving turkey. I pulled against her pull and the best I could since my right arm was bandaged due to recovering from elbow surgery. The bone was slippery, I couldn't get a tight grip, and the little half broke off in my hand. I still made my wish, not remembering at the moment that your wish is supposed to come true only if you come up with the large end of the wishbone.

With that, memories of wishbones of the past came flooding back to me. What I remember is seeing Bernie earnestly at the kitchen table, painting the wishbone with red fingernail polish. She would paint the wishbone like she did her own nails, slow, deliberate, and careful, finishing each stroke of the brush with a sense of finality. I remember how she would then hang the dried painted wishbone on a nail behind the kitchen stove. That's where the memory ended, so I reached out to my sisters, via text, to see what they remembered, and here are their responses:

My first question, 6:10 pm: "Hey, do ya'll remember when Bernie would paint the wishbone from the turkey? I remember telling Nicole and she thought it was weird."

6:20, Evette: "I don't remember anything about that."

6:30, Carolyn: "Wishbone steps: Cut around the breast portion and remove it to make sure no one broke the wishbone before carving the turkey. Clean and wash the wishbone. Sit it in the window to dry overnight. She sat at the kitchen table and painted it without distraction the next evening or so. Then she hung it on the nail on the left side of the stove next to that 1956 white and gold-trimmed honeymoon plate from Niagara Falls. It seemed like a very long time till she decided to make a wish, and one of us would wish with her and whoever got the biggest part of the wishbone was happy because their wish was supposed to come true. I was mesmerized by that ritual and remember being the one on the other end while wishing and breaking that bone on a few occasions."

6:34, me: "I remember that exactly as you said, minus a few intricate details! Thank you! I was on the end of that bone break too! I wonder what we all wished for."

6:41, Carolyn: "Me too. It was funny how she included one of us on the other end. I guess whoever was nearest her at the time had a wish time."

6:42, me: "I didn't think it was weird. I understand her artistic nature side, and perhaps the kid in her had so much to wish for or pray for."

6:44, Brenda: "Gee whiz, you all have amazing memories... I remember too...the plate, the breaking, but not all those details. Thank you, Divas, for the memories. Maybe she wished for peace and happiness, healing for Lil Lind and Granny. We will never know, but I know we all miss her and that is why I think Jewels had this memory in the first place. I was sad at Thanksgiving again because it reminded me of her cancer diagnosis the day after, but it's all good...bittersweet memories are all right."

6:53, Carolyn: "It's funny because every time I see a turkey I think of how I would ask her about that other little bone in the turkey that resembles the wishbone and she used to show me the difference."

6:54, me: "I know! Now I am dancing in the living room to her playing the piano! I am going to take what I have and write our book, for real, this time!"

6:55, Carolyn: "Love it! I was thinking the same type of wishes and prayers, too. It's great to replace sad memories with good ones."

6:59, Carolyn: "Yes, I still remember coming from Wisconsin up to the hospital that day after Thanksgiving in 1996. I bathed her while you and Jewels were talking with the doctors."

7:04, Brenda: "There is that memory again...yes. I see Jewels right next to me, while I felt the floor disappear from under me, and it got dark and I couldn't ... I think I was gonna faint, but God kept me. Yes.... the book, I was thinking about it this morning."

7:10, Carolyn: "Me too. I can't wait till I get in my own place so I can organize my writing again. My computer is still in storage, but I started organizing my sister letters again from my emails."

7:11, Marilyn: "Hate to be Debbie Downer, but I have no thoughts about the wishbone or hospital or any of those memories y'all share. I just remember seeing it, the wishbone."

7:16, Carolyn: "That is okay. You have your own memories, and that makes great sister letters, because we all have our own memories. If you only knew how powerful your letters could be to the whole, we'd already have one book. You should write some more letters for the sister book."

7:16, me: "That is not a downer because now you have the memories because we are sharing them."

7:18, Marilyn: "But knowing Bernie, it had a great deal to do with her upbringing. Mama did the wishbone thing too—she just did not paint it, but removed it."

7:19, Carolyn: "How did you feel about the wishbone? Did you ever ask Bernie, What is that?' That is a letter or a response."

7:19, Brenda: "And everybody remembers the wishbone, our mother's symbol of hope that wishes can come true, and we can make some of ours happen. Maybe in 2015 we can start the letter rotation again, Book 2, since Jewels is going on with what we have."

7:20, Carolyn: "So maybe it was a ritual passed down—wow!"

7:22, Brenda: "Yes...wow!"

7:26, Marilyn: "I guess that was a childhood thing that children did. Our mother was special in her own loving way, and her way of expressing herself was amazing and had a certain innocence in it, as well."

7:30, Carolyn: "You are so right. Write that letter. We would have never known Mama also did the wishbone thing till you said so."

7:35, Marilyn: "I used to break it and wish by myself. I never broke it with her or nothing like that. She told me about the wishbone and the wishing part. Mamma would have never done that. I don't know to this day that she did any of the fun things Bernie did. That was not in her character."

7:36, Brenda: "Yes and that is our heritage. I am out y'all, crashing from the Sunday adrenaline rush... Smooches."

This is the conversation I remember that occurred between the doctor, Brenda, and me, out of earshot of our mom...

Brenda or me to the doctor: "So did you find out what is wrong with her?"

Doctor, looking surprised: "You don't know?"

I Wonder What She Wished For

Us: "Know what?"

We moved into the hallway at this point, where she told us that our mother had pancreatic cancer and she was unlikely to live past six months. There it was, blunt, out in the open, with no in-between. She went on to say that even though chemotherapy could be an option, it would just delay her demise, as the cancer had already metastasized to her liver.

I went from an after Thanksgiving visit to bring her one of her favorite things, food, to all of a sudden finding out that she will probably not be there next Thanksgiving, which came as a surprise and shock, even though deep down I knew Bernie was very sick. This became most evident to me when she tasted the stuffing I had made for Thanksgiving and said, "Ugh, this is nasty, Julie. What you do to it?" I came to later realize that was her way of refusing food and saving face at the same time. I stood up for my stuffing, a recipe that she loved, that I have made for years. She was the only one who said they didn't like it!

Bernie died on March 12, 1997, and she was buried on March 19, 1997, an unseasonably warm and sunny day. I remember when we got to the cemetery for the service that the sun began to shine brightly. I then remembered her saying that when spring comes she will feel better. Well, spring came and she did feel better because she discarded that cancer-ridden body of hers.

With love,
Jewels

Kevin and Brenda

CHAPTER 4
Hero Child

Hero: A person who, in the opinion of others, has special achievements, abilities, or personal qualities, and is regarded as a role model or ideal

"Do not forsake wisdom, and she will protect you; love her, and she will watch over you."
—Proverbs 4:6

FEBRUARY 2013

Hey Divas,

Carolyn's mention in her last letter of being the middle sister had me thinking all weekend about my position in the birth order of our family. Being the oldest birthed from the marriage of my parents put me in the position of being the "hero child."

I did not know what that meant (hero child) or the implications of it until I began college courses at the age of thirty-five.

By then, I had lived out the role and was recovering from the pain of being in that position. This is a book in itself, but sharing just a few thoughts, what first comes to mind is how lonely that position was. I thought about being in the middle for Carolyn and how that may feel like support on both sides, but this is my impression, not hers.

The hero child, for me, meant at the head of the line, with no one to lean on in front of me and a whole lot of responsibility following after me (my siblings). That is why children in my position tend to be and feel overly responsible, something that I still struggle with today at almost fifty-eight years old.

I had no confidante among my siblings because I was the "other mother" figure and it was not for me to share my hopes, dreams, and fears with them, and because of the added dysfunction of my family, I needed to try and be there for them so they could share that with me, if they chose to.

I always felt overwhelmed, looking back down the line at each one of them, trying to figure out what they needed, emotionally and practically, and then doing whatever I could to try and supply it. One of the reasons I wanted to be old enough to work is so that I could provide for my siblings, especially after our father died and needing things such as food and clothes became a reality in our lives. In a sense, I tried to be the mother and the father at different points in our lives.

It was such a lonely existence as a child, but I remember I always had a keen sense of the fact that "someone" was there. It was not an imaginary playmate, because I did not have a real childhood (another result of being in that position), but it was a "presence" that I could feel. This presence brought peace and calm when I gathered my sisters and brothers together to shield them from the violence of our parents' bloody fights, and this presence kept me steady so I could hold back my tears because if I cried then they would be more afraid.

As I look back, I realize now that this presence was with me all the time, but I did not talk to it because I knew it could hear everything inside my head and heart. This presence assured me that everything was going to be all right and it did not matter that I did not have anyone in front of me to lean on or behind me to hold me up when I felt weak because it surrounded me on every side and I was protected. I knew I would be able to stand in my position regardless of what would come our way. I thank God for His presence. I didn't even know Him. But He has always been there.

"And He said, My Presence will go with you, and I will give you rest."

—Exodus 33:14

Peace and Love,
Lil Diva

Divas,

It is so awesome to address the roles we played as children...and stair-steps at that. So close in age, but age is just a number.

I remember being the older child in number, a kind of a get in where you fit in, but because the position was taken, I just got in line, following suit. I thought I was supposed to do something, but what? I knew that the hero was present, and I think because I just wanted to be around, to be connected, just being that was okay.

Diva Five Alive

I first encountered the hero when I came over and our mother had been beaten. I did not know of the abuse, had no clue. She was sitting next to our mother on the bed in the back room. She looked up at me and I saw tears, fear and compassion all in one glance. Did I know what to do? No. Did I know what to say? No. But she rubbed our mother's face and her hair and was present for her—that's the hero I knew.

Those times we laughed so hard and her forgetting her role for a moment was unforgettable, but she was a force that could not be stopped, so I had little to do as Big Sis because I had a hero to do it. Like a lioness protecting her cubs, like an eagle flying high keeping a watchful eye, you are my hero. I hope this made sense, as so much is in my head right now.

So there you have it,
Big Diva

Hey Divas,

When Carolyn first said she was the middle sister, I thought she meant she was the middle child, and then I thought, what is she talking about? I am the middle child! I have always thought of myself as the middle child of the children from my mother, as I have four older siblings (the oldest brother is deceased) and four younger siblings, so where I sit, I am the middle child. Carolyn, of course, is the middle sister—I will give her that.

I have at times thought about what it meant to be a middle child, but have not put much stake in that because to be a child in our family, whether you were the middle, the youngest, or the oldest, did not afford you the opportunity to escape the wrath or the turmoil of living in such dysfunction, where alcohol, drug, and child abuse was the order of the day.

When I reflected upon the letter Brenda wrote, I had memories of the things she mentioned. I remember her working at the phone company and helping to support the family. I remember her buying pretty dressers and colorful comforters and sheets from the mail-order store Aldens, to spruce up the room where the four of us girls slept.

I remember her coming home from the phone company one day, looking cute in a nice outfit, and my mother was standing on the porch and said to her, "You bitch, you think you are something because you got a job." I remember feeling hurt for her.

I remember the day she was crying when Carolyn had a sickle cell crisis, saying, "I wish it was me, instead of her." I remember how she would often break out in hives probably because of the stress of living in such a crazy house.

I remember her cooking dinner for the family when Bernie had left us and how one time she let me "season the meat" and I over-salted it, but she told me that it was okay.

I remember how she came to my rescue in the form of pulling a knife on Marilyn because of Marilyn's verbal and almost physical attack on me because I did not change Maurice's diapers when she was gone. I remember reaching for that knife to stop her, and when she pulled it back, it sliced my finger. I remember walking to Community Hospital alone to get stitches, taking with me the cardboard container that held five dollars of quarters, which she gave to me as a way to say she was sorry for cutting me.

I also have memories of how, as a younger sister, I looked to this "hero child" for guidance and support, which was often misdirected during our childhood. I remember always wanting to get her approval. I thought how I would love to paint my nails how she did and how I was thrilled when she finally taught me. I remember being honored to roll her hair, only to be cursed out because I did not do it right. I remember her putting dishwashing detergent in my cereal because of her apparent dislike of me. I remember her buying Evette a new outfit, but not bringing one home for me, and the hurt I felt. I remember her scratching my face with her long nails and asking me to cover it up so that my father would not see it.

I remember when I had my first boyfriend who was becoming distant, so I sought her advice. She informed me that I needed to have sex with him because that was why he was distant. I remember after having sex with him, how in the presence of grown men (friends of my mother's), she told me, "You think you hot shit now that you're fucking." I remember being embarrassed to no end of the disclosure of my sex life. I remember that first sexual encounter and how my mother caught us and her response was, "Your Jones is bigger than Tim's," making reference to my boyfriend's penis being bigger than her boyfriend's. I remember the embarrassment and the lie I told her afterwards, that I was on the pill, because she had told us all that "if y'all start fucking, ya'll better get on the pill." Those are my memories, minus whatever place I fell in the family.

Fast-forward to years present and my discovery of God and His saving grace and His ability to restore relationships. Thanks be to Him that "hero child" is today my true hero, someone I can count on to pray for me, to tell me the truth, to uplift me, and to be there for me to share my innermost thoughts and feelings, which I don't often do, and to encourage me and remind me to always keep God first.

I thank God that my true oldest sister, Marilyn, has acknowledged that she wants to take her place as the oldest. I thank God that Carolyn is still living and thriving, even with sickle cell disease. I thank God that Evette is willing to share her stories, as well. And the beat goes on!

With love,
Jewels

Hey Divas,

I don't know who dubbed the title "hero child," but that is exactly what my sister who is just thirteen months older than me was (and at times still is) to our entire clan.

After suffering so many beat downs at the hands of our father, our mother left home for at least two years and didn't return until our dad was at the Veterans Hospital. I remember my hero child comforting our mother after the abuse. As kids we grew to learn that the mood in the house was dictated by how our dad felt and not by what our mother did. I thought she was a great mother and a great housekeeper when we were younger.

During the late afternoon hours, our hero child would watch the clock and run across the alley to "Aunt Pollie's," our neighbor and our mother's drinking buddy, to make her come home and sober up before our dad got home, usually around 6:00 p.m. on Tuesday and Thursday evenings. Everyone dreaded Dad's early nights, as he ate dinner with us. We had to eat all of our vegetables and not speak at the dinner table. These dinner nights with our dad felt like an eternity.

On one occasion, I remember our mother was tipsy, our hero child not having been able to sober her up in time. Our dad had come home with groceries and she was putting the groceries away, and just out of the blue, as she took the quart-size Heinz Apple Cider Vinegar out of the brown paper bag, and before she could sit the vinegar on the table and empty the remaining groceries from the bag, he picked it up and used her head as a post to break it on.

I remember how she immediately fell back and the dazed look in her eyes. Everything happened so quickly, but I still saw it all, all in a flash, our hero child being there to soothe our mother's head with ice, and a towel. She did all she could do under the wrath and anger of our father. As our mother's head swelled, and she cried, and we all screamed, our hero child continued to nurse her wounds, holding her head close to her chest, as if she was the mother.

The house we grew up in was filled with violence and blood, screaming and nervous tension. Our three brothers learned how to deal with the tension by bumping their heads on the sofa, all in a row. They would rock and bump, rock and bump, and the higher the tension in the house, the worse their nerves, and the harder they would bump. In fact, they bumped their heads so much they left impressions in that green sofa, marking their spots for its lifetime. All three in a row claimed their spot, night after night, and our middle brother bumped his head even as an adult.

I also remember many fights, but the knife fight that left our mother's right thumb hanging by the skin was the bloodiest I'd ever seen as a child. I thought my mother withstood so much pain. When I looked at her face, she had a void look, as if her spirit had left her body. I don't remember anything but blood and screams from all of us, but somehow my mother got to the hospital and got stitched up. I don't remember if the police or the ambulance was called that particular time, but I always remember my dad telling war stories with the officers and laying down the law with whoever was in authority, saying, "This is my house and I ain't goin' nowhere."

The abuse continued, and our hero child was always there to pick up the pieces. She acted as a bridge between our raging dad and our mother, protected us when we saw the violent fights, and wiped our mother's wounds, and then read to our younger siblings on the sofa or sitting around that coffee table in the living room. However, our mother didn't start off, from my remembrance, being a heavy drinker. In fact, I realized all she really liked later on in life was "Schultz that's it" beer and later on Schultz Malt Liquor. I think she drank to forget her problems and abuse.

My hero also gave me assignments. I remember one time she burned the pork chops. They must have been expensive because our dad was mad. He yelled at my hero and told her, "Well, let Carolyn cook if she can do a better job." I often was assigned to cook at least the meat for dinner, doing my share of whatever it took to keep some semblance of peace and order in the house.

Another assignment that I did not mind at the time, but haunts me to this day, was disciplining my brothers and baby sister. Floyd especially reminds me of how I use to discipline him worse than Big Lind (our father). He told me as recent as two years ago, "You use to take me on the back stairwell and take my head and bump it against the wall, and I hated it when you did that. You were so mean, and Brenda use to let you hit us." When he said that, I kindly corrected him, saying, "She didn't let me hit you—it was my assignment to discipline you guys—you, Michael, Kevin, and Evette—because you guys didn't listen to her. It was her way, and my way, of keeping you all in line, to keep you from throwing rocks at cars, digging up mud ditches on the side of the yard, and making and eating mud pies. My hero and I together were trying to prevent you from doing what you shouldn't be doing and save you kids from the wrath of our father.

How we discipline our children today is really different from how we were disciplined as children. I apologized, but I told Floyd, "I only did what I learned." There were no domestic violence laws when we were kids. Or if there were, my father didn't obey them.

And, in fact, I wasn't mean. Most times, I was living, breathing, and walking in daily pain, my hero being the only one besides my mother who understood my pain.

My illness would frighten my younger siblings, and at most I got attention from everyone, but they didn't know how to take care of me. I think my illness would shape the whole household at times. I thought it determined whether my dad was going to be happy or angry. I thought it determined if my mother was abused or not.

I vividly remember having a really bad "pain crisis" one day, and my hero told our dad, "She needs to go to the hospital, Daddy." And he replied, "Let her die." This hurt me so bad, and it stuck with me for many, many years. I have a high tolerance for pain because I learned to withstand all types of suffering as a child, just as all my siblings did. For my genetic disorder, sickle cell anemia, Bayer aspirin was the strongest at-home remedy my mother knew of when I was a kid. My hero knew it too, and she also knew when I was feeling really bad and it was time for me to go to the hospital. As a child, she learned how to take care of me and comfort me too in our mother's absence.

I don't know if it was the job at Marshall Field's, the change purses full of dimes, the boyfriend who hung over the fence who was dared to cross over by our dad standing in the door just in his boxers, or our hero cursing at our dad, or our cousin, Leslie, calling him Pickles because he was being unreasonable, or the fact that we were both little mothers and growing older, but our hero seemed to have more power over the household and allowed us more freedom than we had ever known. I don't know what it was, or if our hero really had that effect on the household, or if Pickles was completely losing his will to live, but I think all of the above had an effect, but the later was taking place, too.

I remember once coming home from middle school and Pickles was home alone in the middle of the afternoon. I thought this was strange because he always worked until the evening or late at night. He was sitting in the chair in the right corner of the living room, rocking and gazing out of the window. Before I could reach the kitchen, I smelled gas so strong it was making me sick. I didn't think anything was wrong, but all the knobs on the stove were turned on and nothing was lit, so I turned the knobs off. I asked our dad, "Daddy, didn't you smell that gas?" He didn't even look at me directly. I went into our bedroom, off the kitchen, wondering where everyone was, as no one else seemed to be home. Then I went back into the kitchen and the gas knobs were all on again. I was really scared, as no one, not even our hero, was home at the time.

 I remember leaving out the back door quietly and running all the way through the alley to my friend, Dorothy's, house. I don't really remember all the details, but I knew something had happened to my dad. We were all at someone else's house, and I ended up staying with her family until the day our mother came back home. A few days later, I learned our dad was in the hospital, and he never came back to us. At that point, life living with our mother took off on a different course. She came home, but she was different. We were smoking and telling her that she couldn't do anything about it. A couple of years after that, my hero changed, and when my hero left, I guess I missed her so much I changed too, but that's another story in itself.

 When I grew older (and got sober), I reflected back on my life, our life, and I think our dad loved us the best he knew how. I remember the Saturday and Sunday outings, the days at Lincoln Park Zoo, the rides in the country, sitting in the back of that big blue 1956 Impala car, thinking we were rich because my legs didn't reach the floor.

 I remember the picnics and barbecues at the Forest Preserve, where we would stay until dusk. I remember the smells of my mother, my father, of barbecue and watermelon, and the taste of Orange Crush Soda, and how our dad was generous with whomever he encountered. I remember him keeping a big metal open cooler in the trunk of his car filled with ice and sodas, perhaps beer and liquor too. I remember even a stranger could get a cool drink and free car repairs. I remember the date nights our parents took to Riverside Amusement Park and how happy our mother would be sometimes.

I remember Christmases with the silver tree and the multi-colored spinning wheel that created shadows and colors all over the walls. I remember presents that covered the entire living room. I remember the piano being filled with trays of Christmas ribbon candies and other goodies. And I remember Sambo and the whole hams, and our dad closing the sliding door when they sat around the kitchen table on a Sunday afternoon, trading war stories or talking about things too delicate for our ears.

As I reflect back, I also remember thinking that perhaps our dad did suffer from some type of mental illness. I think about our missing sister often and how she too suffers from mental illness. Did he? Do we all? Whatever the circumstances, I know life is full of pain and pleasures, and I know that violence does have long-term effects. There were no laws against domestic violence when we were children. I can't look at a bottle of Heinz Vinegar without remembering the violence inflicted upon our mother. I couldn't look at our mother's thumb when she was alive without remembering the knife and all that blood, but I can reflect back and thank God we are all survivors, thank God for being a Great Deliverer, and thank God that I have older sisters today who I can still look up to.

Straight from the heart,
Sadie

Hey Divas,

As I was reading my sister's letter, all kinds of visions came before me, and for the first time I wasn't afraid to face them. I can remember one violent scene when Big Lind took the bottle and hit my momma on the head with it. I remember feeling like it was my fault because he told me to take the groceries out of the bag, and I remember my mom sitting in the chair watching as he picked up the bottle. He raised it as though he was going to hit me, but he hit her instead. For a long time, I thought he only picked on me, and I was told by him I was too dark to be his child. I didn't know back then what I was feeling as I was too young, but I know I was confused and remember being afraid and not liking that man at all.

Yeah Big Sis, I will never forget when you took me shopping and bought me clothes for school. I was in high school at the time and didn't have many clothes. But I was determined to go to school no matter what people were saying about me. A long blue jeans coat was out then, and when you bought that for me, I remember thinking, she is the best sister in the world!

I realize now that we all remember different things that happened in our lives and we are not far apart in age. I just realized, writing this letter, I referred to Bernie as Mom, and I can't say I ever remember calling her Mom, and for me, that's a feeling taking place, something a doctor can't heal, but through this letter writing with my sisters, I feel this is going to bring a lot of healing. I love you all. And thank you Lord.

Love,
Ms. Evette

Carolyn, Julie and Marilyn

CHAPTER 5
Relationships

"Wounds from a friend may be trusted, but an enemy multiplies kisses."

—Proverbs 27:6

MARCH 2013

Hey Divas,

First, I want to start off by saying that relationships are overrated and there is way too much made of them and way too much hurt surrounding them. As a child, my relationships with my grandmother and grandfather were different, as one was present and one was not, meaning all the attention came from Grandpa, and I loved him, but there is not much to say about him because he did not say a whole lot. He was more about action, and the time I spent with him, I remember fishing, and catching worms. He let me help sell the fish, too. I remember being so excited.

We talked and laughed a lot. I remember he peeled apples in one whole peel and it was so amazing to me. He amazed me and his strength was so awesome. He was a strong man and very smooth and might I add handsome, very Indian-looking. I am talking about him because he was in my life for a short time and I really missed him when he was gone. I cried a lot and did not understand.

I think Mama felt sorry for me as she was not at all the lovey-dovey type. She was stern and very soft-spoken, and I had two very different relationships with her and my grandfather. She was just Mama, and she loved me, but I had a hard time trying to figure it out. So growing up, I looked up to Grandpa really for the dad I never had.

The relationship with my family, my sisters and brothers, was the weirdest, but I loved them, my mother too. I don't know if I really understand all of it to this day. I know we grow and learn from our experiences. I learned that not all people are going to return love to you the way you want it. I know that all people have a purpose in your life, the ones that cross your path, and I know that some will really hurt you. I know hurt and pain from neglect of people, from not knowing who I really was, and letting people live in my head too long. I am venting right now, so if I go off-subject, chalk it up to my poor attention span!

I loved being in love with Big Maurice and Stan. They loved me—no pretense; it was real. In that, I received a love child, who is in love with his family, and loves people, a gift from my lover man—that's what I called Big M. back then. But, all in all, their love was different for different times—that's what the key is, the timing. I am so glad I have a loving family, and loving siblings. Even though I missed out on really knowing my dad, or really feeling his love, I had some real love guys in my life. They did not make up for Grandpa's, but it was love just the same, and they loved the best they knew how.

So there you have it,
Big Diva

Hey Divas,

I don't believe relationships are overrated. I believe that God means for people to be in relationship with each other. I do agree that, as Big Diva said, there is a lot of hurt and pain involved in relationships. I have been thinking about this lately as I struggle in my own personal relationships. I am thinking, what is really at the root of my low self-esteem, my self-doubt? I am sure a lot of it has to do with the so-called daddy issues, but most of the time I think "time-out" for all that. No excuses, you are a woman, make your mind up that you are going to believe that you are great and worthy of wonderful, reciprocal relationships. I am working on that. I am happy to be in relationship with my sisters and am so grateful that we are able to share our stories.

I remember the times I would go to Bethel and was always so proud to see a window dedicated to my grandfather. I would often wonder what he looked like, etc., but had no memories I could pull up, as I think I was two when he passed away. When I read Big Diva's letter, I saw him through her eyes, the "Indian look," the smoothness of the man and the way he treated his grandbaby. I saw the apple peel fall off the apple in one whole unbroken piece and thought, how cool was that! Wow, thank you, Big Diva, for introducing me to the grandfather I never knew.

I am sorry for how his loss affected you. I think about what my paternal grandfather must have been thinking when he went into the barn and committed suicide by shooting himself in the head. I wonder what was hurting him so bad. I think how it would have been nice to know a grandfather.

I am beginning to realize that as a child I don't think I even realized that Marilyn was being raised by our grandparents. How weird that must have felt when her siblings had a home with a mother (her mother, as well) and a father.

Anyway, I am not giving up on love. I am going to be praying that God will give me a man like my grandpa, the one I saw through Marilyn's eyes, someone to spend time with, to talk to and laugh with, someone with "strength, awesome and handsome," someone who "amazes" me, but most of all, someone who loves God. I am sure that is why my grandfather had that window in the church—he loved God and must have been dedicated to God's work. Happy Resurrection Sunday! He lives!

With love,
Jewels

Divas,

The older I get, and I am a year older at the writing of this letter, the more I realize how important relationships are. I think I have always longed for closer family relationships and real girlfriend relationships all my life. One of the sacrifices of me not having a regular job and living away is struggling to maintain close relationships with family and friends. My position in the birth order, along with my natural loner tendency, allowed me to get along in life without them, until I got sober and saved.

Then family relationships changed for the better—praise God! It was like the light came on and I could finally see my mother, sisters, and brothers, the immediate family, for what seemed like the first time.

I could really feel love without being under the influence of mood- and mind-altering substances, and most of all, God's love filled my heart. The scripture says the love of God is shed abroad in our hearts by the Holy Spirit—amen. Thank God for His Spirit, as it enables me to walk in more ways than in the flesh.

These are some of my thoughts regarding relationships. My memories of Daddy (our maternal grandfather) are faint, but they are there. The most prominent would be me looking at him in the living room on Dodge Street, sitting in a white T-shirt and listening to the old radio, which as best I can recall served more like a television in those days. I don't remember him talking much, but I can also remember him as somewhat stern and he was "red-skinned" and handsome, that Indian blood I guess. Goodness, we are part Indian and Irish, at least on our mother's side, and who knows what else.

My final memory of Daddy is seeing him in the window of Community Hospital. My mother had taken me there and probably another sibling or two also, but I cannot be sure. I just know I was too little to go into the hospital and she said he wanted to see me (us), so we went and he looked out the window, and I remember distinctly him throwing candy out and I picked it up out of the grass. To my recollection, I never saw him again. I don't believe he left that hospital, I do know he had heart trouble, and I also remember how much our mother loved her father.

I remember the apple peeling, and that somebody else could peel one long unbroken peel—it was either Mama or our Aunt Johnnie. I remember eating the peelings on the front porch on Dodge Street. Apples tasted so much better in those days. But now you better not eat the peels because you would be ingesting pesticides.

Finally, I see Big Diva laughing with Daddy. I think he was tickling her. And yes, they had a special relationship. I remember wishing I had it with him too, but I didn't, and it was okay, because even then as a child, I realized that family members interacted differently with one another. And the same holds true today, and it's all right. We love each other just the same.

It's great to have memories of family—the good, the bad, and the ugly. All of them are a part of who we are, whether we experienced the memory or it was just passed on to us. As we share our memory pieces with each other, somehow I feel like it is making us whole.

I believe that relationships are the keys to life, first with God, then with yourself (gotta love you), and finally with others.

Till next time...

Peace and Love,
Lil Diva

Divas,

The most dreadful thing that I found out about myself is that I believed everyone deserved to be happy but me. I continued to punish myself with this thought, people pleasing, per say, until it wore me into a corner, where I came face to face with my own demons. Where did I learn to people please? I learned to people please by covering up the realities of my life as a child.

"What goes on in this house stays in this house" is the message I heard over and over when I was growing up. So by not opening up and telling another, or even having a chance to tell another, I was not able to express how I felt bruised and battered and unloved, when I deserved love, how misunderstood I felt, when all I wanted was to be understood. I was not able to express how ashamed I was of my own mother when she walked down Church Street butt-naked when she thought she was Jesus Christ. Everyone in school knew, making me feel ashamed to face my peers because of my crazy home life. That's how I learned how to people please, thinking, oh my, we are the only ones in the whole world that are so dysfunctional.

I had to please everyone whom I thought was important to me or better than me. I am not important, or so I thought. I have to take care of home. I have to make my dad his oyster soup to get rid of his hangovers. I have to watch over my mother—I can't leave her because she might die from a seizure. I have to do right, so everyone will be happy. I cannot afford to be sick; I want everything to be okay. I have to please my lover, who beat me down and told me I was nothing. I didn't know that I was beautiful and deserved to be loved and receive love too. I know when I would try to people please, I'd let people, especially those who hurt me, live in my head too long, if you know what I mean, like Big Diva stated.

In recovery, I finally found out that I could love in a relationship freely without expectations of others. When I give of myself freely, then I am free to love and forgive in return. This type of love frees me up from people pleasing and worrying about if others love me or not.

For a long time, I had this wall up where I would not even entertain deep relationships, not even with my own family members, because I was tired of being hurt. Once I learned to forgive and forget and accept people as they were and not try to change what I could not change about other people, I found myself to be a happier person and free to accept the differences in each person

I encountered. I often heard the saying that some people are in your life for a reason, a season, or a lifetime.

I often wondered why Marilyn and even Lynn would not come and live with us all the time. I remember how much fun it was when they would come, even if it was for a day or just an hour, how Big Diva would always be dressed to kill in her pretty lace socks and big pigtails. As I grew older, I wondered if Momma just wanted to keep Marilyn to herself or if she could not live with us because of our dad's decision. I really did not realize for a long time that they were our sisters too. I used to think Marilyn belonged to Momma and Lynn was my father's daughter who lived through the alley. I only knew she resembled our dad so much that she had to be his relative. Anyhow, I thought they were special friends, like gifts to cherish and make us happy.

It was my former pastor's wife who taught me how to accept gifts from others without thinking I owed them something in return. She said, "Sister Gibert, when someone gives you a gift, that is because they love you, and not because they expect something in return." After she told me this many years ago, I began a journey of finding out what was wrong with me. I didn't even think I was good enough to receive a gift from someone, even after, when I look back, I did something special to deserve the gift. She said, "A simple thank you is good enough or a card in the mail thanking the person for the gift." This is an example of how God puts people in your life for a reason. That reason was to teach me how to find worth in myself.

I listened when my pastor recently stated that when Jesus was on the cross and Jesus' mother and family members and his disciples were gathered around the cross, Jesus said to his disciples, "Behold, my mother." He did not say it to his family members, but to his trusted disciple, John. Why? Because he trusted John to take care of his mother over and above the rest of his family. I say this because God always shows up with a friend. No matter how alone we may feel at times, God always sends friends or acquaintances into our lives to fill a void. These too are friends and relationships that God put in our lives for a season or a reason.

I often find solace in Big Diva's ability to laugh and make others laugh. I know laughter is good for the soul, but I find it difficult sometimes because I'm such a serious person. My daughter tells me I'm funny sometimes, so I guess I do have that ability to let loose. I guess God makes us all with attributes to complete each other.

I remember being very proud of Daddy seeing his name on that big roundish stone that lies over to the side of the entry to Bethel Church. I used to picture Daddy as a big strong man. I remember when they built the new Bethel Church they honored Daddy by placing that same rock in the same spot outside of the entryway of the new church. On the bright side, your story sparked my own memories of Daddy—the pictures I painted in my mind from stories our mother told me on my own sickbed over and over again, stories that gave me hope and the will to live.

I was told how Daddy loved to hold me, too, because my cheeks were so fat like yours, how he would kiss them raw, and pinch them till I cried. She also told me stories of how Daddy used to take me and sit me in the middle of that car he had and ride me to church between him and Momma. I only remember what she told me on my sickbed, but those were the stories that brought me healing and helped me know I was loved. Those were the stories that made me proud of my grandfather. She also told me she never thought or no one every suspected I'd be sick because I was the biggest baby she birthed. Those were the stories that gave me the will to live, the will to survive.

I do remember Mamma being stern, but loving and caring. It reminds me how much Bernie, our dear mother, was so full of love for people, and how much she loved us, but she did not know how to express love in touch, in hugs and kisses, because this is not how she was loved as a child.

Momma would bring bags of undergarments and hats and gloves for us to wear. I didn't care if they were not new. As a child, all I cared about was that that woman we call Momma must care about us. I would love to see her coming, but she never stayed long; I never remember long visits. Sometimes I did not know how to address her as a child. It was not until I was deep into my addiction that I spent time with Momma every morning. Buddy and I would drop Jocelyn off at Baby Toddlers very early, and I would visit and sit with Momma to have coffee, before I had to leave for work, for over a year.

It was during these times that I learned to love Momma and see her as a Christian woman who loved me (us) anyway, despite my (our) addictions. I couldn't cover it up. She would just offer the doors of the church to me. She would never push. I used to promise her I would come back to church someday, and when she passed away, I was sober. At that time, I was trying to stay sober on my own. And thanks be to God, I was able to keep that promise for a couple of years after her passing.

I have grown spiritually aware of my own past soul sickness. Today, I know I do not have to people please. Today, I know that I am worthy of being loved. Today, I love myself, so I can accept love in return. Today, I make choices about who I allow in my space, in my life, because I have that right. I have learned that some people are in my life for a reason or a season. That reason may be to bring me a fresh prophetic word, like that gentleman who touched me and prayed for me the other day. I didn't know him, had never met him, but God allowed our paths to cross, so that he (Luke was his last name) could send me a message, a verification, straight from God, and that message was that I have a ministry too in me, and that God is not going to allow me to leave this earth until it is taken up and fulfilled.

He mentioned all the desires of my heart when it comes to women and ministry. He told me God hasn't allowed me to have a mate because God wants me to write in order to bring healing to other women. And I know as I write this letter in response to yours that it is so true. It was my mother who first told me that I would never marry. At first, I thought she was being mean to me, but as I got older, I saw that the choices I made regarding relationships were my own doing, and not God sent. Today, I am comfortable whether or not God sends me a mate, and I will never make that choice on my own again.

However, it is relationships in our lives, paths that intertwine, sometimes crossing and sometimes mingling and lingering, that help to mold us and bring direction to our lives that lead us down the road to our own self-discovery. Without relationships, surely we would perish, but relationships are sometimes tough, and when they get tough, these are the times that God wants our undivided attention. He wants us to focus on Him and nothing and nobody else.

Oh, how much of my life did I waste thinking I wasn't good enough, that I had to please others, that others did not love me. Oh, how senseless and useless that was. We are *all* children of the King and if we are children of the King, our God, our Father, and Our Risen Christ, Jesus only wants the best for us—to fill us up where we are empty, to pick us up from the depths of hell when we stumble and fall, to place us on solid ground, where no man, and I mean no man, can turn us around.

I cherish each and all of my siblings. I understand today that my relationship with one sibling may be totally different from my relationship with another sibling, and when a jealous thought or negative feeling crosses my mind, I'm now aware that these are tricks of the enemy. I just thank God that He gave me so many siblings to love and to have hope in and to confide in. I do not worry about best friends today, and I do not worry about if someone likes me today, because Jesus is my best friend and my rock and all of my siblings are dynamic forces in my life.

I love you guys—I love my brothers, I love my nieces and nephews, I love my cousins and my second, third, and fourth cousins, I love my great-nieces and -nephews, I love my aunts and uncles and my great-aunts and -uncles—I love everyone. And most of all, I love the fact that I, that we, had a praying grandmother. Thank you Jesus!

Happy Resurrection Day!

Straight from the heart,
Sadie

CHAPTER 6
Church and Holiday Memories

"Bring the fattened calf and kill it. Let's have a feast and celebrate."

—Luke 15:23

FEBRUARY 2013

Hey Divas,

With the passing of Valentine's Day, I began to think about the other upcoming holidays and my childhood memories of them. I remember how much fun it was to make homemade Valentine's Day cards and decorate paper lunch bags to take to school to hold my candy for the candy exchange.

I remember Easter and the new dresses and headbands with flowers on them that fit too tight and always made my head hurt because the teeth of the headband would dig into my scalp. I remember the chore Bernie had of washing and pressing all of our heads. I remember the anticipation of being dressed up and even carrying a little white purse. I remember Easter baskets, which I believe were homemade, and the dying of Easter eggs, all directed by Bernie. I can still smell the vinegar as she mixed different dyes and remember our excitement to get our turn to decorate the eggs. I remember an Easter egg hunt she had for us in the backyard. I remember the Easter speeches at church and how much I hated them because I was so shy. I remember, but am not sure if it was Easter that time, when Brenda recited all the books of the Bible and how impressed all the adults were. I particularly remember one year when I knew for sure I had outgrown Easter

Kevin and Big Lind

baskets, how I woke up to find an Easter polo paddle, which had candy included in it, in the window next to my bed (I slept in the top bunk) and how excited I was. I do believe that Brenda bought that for me. I remember how Bernie could work wonders with one of those things, hitting them sidewise, up, down, between her legs, etc., and for a long time, and how I would get so much joy watching her.

One thing I don't remember is Bernie coming to church with us, which she may have. I am just not sure and don't remember, but I don't ever remember Big Lind coming with us. I think during their good times they sent us to church so they could have their time together. In typing this, I began to wonder if things would have been different if they came to church and worshipped God together as a couple and a family.

Fast-forwarding to the next holiday, which would be Memorial Day. I don't remember much about that one, but I do remember the Fourth of July. I remember thinking that we were the only kids who got new outfits for the Fourth of July, always red, white, and blue clothes. I remember I carried on this tradition with my own kids when they were little, buying them red, white, and blue outfits. I remember one particular Fourth of July Marilyn had a red, white, and blue two-piece hot pants suit, along with sandals that laced up to the knee. I remember the picture she took in the front yard with her hands on her hips, looking stunning and stacked, as they would say back in the day. (I think I still have that picture.) I remember barbecues at the Forest Preserve, where there was usually lots of drinking among the adults and fun for the kids. I remember there were many Fourth of Julys that Bernie burnt the ribs, as she was "toasty" and not watching them.

I remember Halloween and how back then the day before Halloween was called Beggars' Night, which was the night designated for trick-or-treating, and people did not usually go trick-or-treating on the actual holiday of Halloween. I remember decorating large paper shopping bags, to be used for trick-or-treating, and how they were quickly replaced with pillowcases in the later years to hold all of the candy we would walk over to Skokie to get. I remember getting the idea of the pillowcases from Natasha, who loved to eat, laugh, and go trick-or-treating. I will conclude my sister letter with that holiday.

With love,
Jewels

Divas,

I am continually amazed at Jewel's razor-sharp memory as it relates to details of events. I could even smell the vinegar with the Easter egg dye when she described it and see Bernie smiling as she made the homemade baskets, which were less expensive than the pre-made (she said that), and plus she enjoyed doing it. She had a creative zone, and when she was in it, you better not mess with her—it was serious and it probably kept her from going crazy, for real. But I know, above all, she did those things because she loved us. She did not do the hugging and the kissing, but every dyed egg and the infamous Easter egg hunt in the backyard, I definitely remember that. And it was out of love, it had to be, and I guess I need to remind myself of that.

As for going to church, I don't know if Bernie told me or I heard Mama say it, but the words were, "You need to send those kids to church," and she did on every special church holiday and some others that were regular Sundays. I remember always looking forward to those Sundays because they would likely be happier days with less tension in the house.

One of the highlights was that Marilyn might come home with us, and for the most part, I enjoyed that, but sometimes I felt some anxiety, and that was probably because it was my big sister who I really did not know that well. But all that faded once we hit the stage on the coffee table and under the light near the front door, where we sang and danced our hearts out. Marilyn was always the best dancer, with those big thick braids swinging in the air.

I remember the food cooking when we came home from church, and it always seemed like we ate late, and I am sure Bernie sipping did not help. She and Big Lind did that on Sunday most times without a fight at the end of the day. And that is another reason I liked Sundays.

I have often thought about reciting the books of the Bible. And it was a memory that was kept alive even when I was trying to die in my addiction. Now I realize that the ability to do that, remember and recite all sixty-six books of the Bible, which I can't even do now as a pastor, without some hesitation, was due to the enabling power of the Holy Spirit. It was God's hand on me early, and I can remember it being easy, very easy, for a child my age, but when I did it, I had an out-of-body experience. I relished the pride on Mama's face, which was still stern, because smiling was not something I can really remember seeing her do. She smiled with her eyes—they kind of twinkled.

I remember Rev. Harrison too, with his twinkling eyes and fire-red face, all that anointing of the Holy Spirit. It was he who christened me when I was a baby—Bernie told me so. And he and his wife loved our mother and treated her like she was their own child. She told me how they used to take her home after church with them and she felt so special. One day the Lord told me that when Rev. Harrison christened me, he gave me to God and prayed for the Lord to use my life, and that, along with divine destination, is why I walk in the office of pastor today—to God be the glory!

I shared this with Uncle J.T. a few years ago, and he said, "Baby, you are probably right—to God be the glory!"

Finally, I remember when Bernie was dying. It sounds so funny to say that, but she was dying those three months and two weeks after the cancer diagnosis. Anyway, one day I asked her about church, why she didn't come with us when we were young, and she said, because Big Lind did not want her to go to church, and she looked so sad. Even now it brings tears to my eyes. All those years of our life, I thought she was being obedient to Mama and sending us because she said to, but she told me she wanted to, but he would not let her.

Now I understand why she was so happy when she started coming to First Church. In the early days, she once came hungover and maybe even drunk with a short dress on and flirted with Pastor Curry. I wanted to crawl under the pew. Now I realize that was the devil. But in the later years, she settled in with her Bible, sitting on the end of the pew, looking over her glasses and smiling when the Spirit got high. She was finally free to worship.

Peace and Love,
Lil Diva

Hey Divas,

Holidays, well, when I think of those, they were great when I was small. It was a lot of cooking Mama did, and all the aunts and uncles were around drunk and talking crazy, but for the most part it was fun. It got to have more meaning getting older when I wanted to spend holidays elsewhere, and even though I was the baby there at Mama's house, it seemed strange, as if something was missing.

I think Uncle Teddy, the baby of the siblings, shared in how I felt. I think he felt neglected or something. I really can't put my finger on it, but I do believe he was kind of like my angel or something, making every holiday magic for me, with gifts and cards. He had this weird connection with me; I think it's because he was the baby, too. He always advocated going to ya'll's house, saying things like, "She needs to grow up with them" and "Let her have fun with her sisters and brothers." I remember one Christmas he brought stuff for you all, and he was more excited than I was.

I just know Easter was my favorite because we went to church for our Easter speeches, and we looked so pretty. We had some really fun holidays, the cookouts, the fishing trips—I miss our holiday stuff.

Fast-forwarding, it's like a part of me is sad about all that. But nevertheless, we have our memories, and that will be in my heart forever.

So there you have it,
Big Diva

Divas,

While reading Jewel's letter, it brought back memories of all those holidays she spoke about. I could feel the smile on my face as I was reading her letter. Oh how I remember having to get dressed up for Easter, wearing those socks with those ruffles on them, folded down by my ankles, and not liking them very much, because my legs were so skinny. I can remember Carolyn being sick and couldn't go to school, and when we came home, she had made us all a Valentine's card or something to do with Valentine's Day.

Like I said, I was smiling as I was reading Jewel's letter because I remember the good times we did have as a family. It was not always bad. As I end this letter to all my lovely sisters, I remember the holidays we spent together.

Love,
Ms. Evette

OCTOBER 2014

Hey Divas,

I believe I was the originator of the sister letter last Halloween, but in an effort to stay present, I did not check to see. "Trick-or-treat, smell my feet, give me something good to eat!" is a phrase that came to mind as I remember those fun times as a kid getting ready to go on the candy hunt.

    I especially remember Natasha, who loved to eat and loved this time of year, because she could go after all the candy she wanted. I remember it was her who suggested we walk across the bridge to Skokie, where the white people would leave their pumpkins and other baskets on their porches filled with candy, trusting that the neighborhood kids would just take one or two pieces. I remember the joy of going to porch after porch, dumping all of the contents of the baskets into pillowcases (which were Natasha's idea) we carried on our backs and running away in glee, laughing so hard I almost peed on myself on many occasions. Gosh, those were fun and simple times, which, as I sit here typing my letter, I miss.

    This Halloween is approaching with the uncertainty of my future. With the upcoming loss of a job and a consistent income, I am left with the stark reality that I am not a happy-go-lucky kid anymore who only has to worry about the next porch from which she would fill her pillowcase full of candy, but am reminded of the weight of that candy, once that pillowcase got full, and how I had to carry it all the way back across the bridge and how the load was not as light as it was when I set off on my journey. That is kind of how I feel now, as my load is kind of heavy and I am wondering how I will make it across that bridge. But just like I did as a child, with that pillowcase full of candy, I will make it across, one step at a time, stopping often to rest.

With love,
Jewels

Divas,

Since Jewels stopped at Halloween, I feel the need to continue starting with Thanksgiving. This was one of my favorite holidays. I can remember Bernie in the kitchen cooking and how I would love to watch and eventually help her. I remember when I used to stick the cloves in the ham and how I would grate the cheese for the macaroni. I remember how Bernie used to spread the brown paper bag on the table and clean the chitterlings. And this one time, I was helping her, I scraped a lump and it burst into my face. Oh how I cried because of the smell, and I swore I would never help do that again. And I can't say if I ever did.

Moving on to Christmas, I remember on Christmas Day, our living room would be filled from the front window to the kitchen door with toys. How I remember Cuddly Dudley, though I don't know if one particular person got him, or if he was all of ours.

In writing this letter, I remember how, as brothers and sisters, in our younger years, we had fun together, but I don't ever remember seeing Big Lind and Bernie having fun together. I'm not saying they didn't, but I just don't remember. It makes me sad at times that all I can remember is Big Lind not being nice to us, at all. Yeah, he provided for us, but that doesn't make up for the things he did to our family. Well anyway, I am so glad my story is being told.

Love,
Ms. Evette

Hey Divas,

As I read Evette's letter, I could see her chocolate-colored legs, all greasy with Vaseline, with those lacy socks turned down, feet in either white or black patent-leather shoes. Her story about the chitterlings is funny and nasty at the same time. I remember wanting to please Bernie and feeling so honored when she would let me help with the cooking. I do believe that she had special times for each of us to help her, as I never remember more than one of us helping her with dinner at one time. I also remember sticking cloves in the ham and how I would try to be so precise doing that.

I also remember helping to clean chitterlings, and as much as I hated the smell, I loved to be able to work side by side with my mom. She would scrap the chitterling first and then pass it to me to clean it more. I remember her saying that you should be able to see through the really thin ones if you scraped them right. I would hold them up to the light when I was done to see if I could see through them.

I don't ever remember her being impatient with me as I helped her cook. I sure did not inherit that trait and did not look forward to my girls helping me in the kitchen. I think that is because I am

Church and Holiday Memories

so hyper and did not have the patience to work with someone's learning curve. I think Bernie liked to cook. I can remember the special treats of steaks on some Saturday nights and how the smell of them mixed with the sound of Perry Mason would reach my nostrils and my ears.

I know the Cuddly Dudley was for Kevin, and I think I remember Bernie and Big Lind getting him free from a bank. I think a bank was having a promotion for opening up accounts and the Cuddly Dudley was the promotion prize. When I think about how stressful it must have been for Bernie and Big Lind to raise us and to provide for us, it is just amazing to me. Some people can't even do that with one child! Cooking for us was like cooking for a small army, not including cleaning up after us and washing all those dishes, because we sure did not have a dishwasher back in those days.

As March marks the anniversary of Bernie's death, I am so thankful to be able to have all of these fond memories, because there was a time when I could only remember the bad things she did and I had a lot of anger toward her. I know she is looking down smiling at us for doing this project, so I want to say to her: "Thank you for being an awesome mom and for imparting your legacy to me. I love you!"

Until we meet again...

With love,
Jewels

Hey Divas,

I was just thinking about how as children we want what we want and have no idea what it takes to get it. Children tend to be selfish because they are children and haven't gained knowledge of what it means to be a responsible adult. They have no idea what it takes for their parents to feed and clothe them and keep a roof over their heads. All they understand is what they need: new clothes, toys, school supplies, lunch money, Christmas presents, field trip money, Girl Scout dues, new Easter dresses, shoes, and purses. In a large family such as ours, we did learn that things cost, so we all started earning money for what we needed early in life.

But as very young children, we made lists for Santa Claus, in whom I never believed, because at a young age, Bernie let me see her wrapping presents, and I also helped. "Hand me the tape, give me the scissors, put this one in that pile"—she was never frazzled, because present wrapping, like everything else she did, was completely organized. I am sure our mother had a little OCD, and maybe that's where I got mine.

Anyway, Cuddly Dudley, the star of the Ray Rayner show, I believe was our baby brother Kevin's gift. But Evette is so right in that he was all of ours, as he sat on the well-lived-on couch like one of us. We all hugged him. We all snuggled with him. I even remember punching him, letting out some childhood anger. But he was Kevin's, Bernadine's youngest son.

I remember that Cuddly Dudley was bigger than Kevin. After a while, Cuddly Dudley's color (I think it was orange) began to fade, and he got a little raggedy, tattered, and dirty and just looked downright bad. But Kevin dragged him around and kept him for a long time. He was his pacifier when he cried himself to sleep bumping his head and clutching his precious Cuddly at the same time. That stuffed dog was just one of the gifts that filled the floor on Christmas, as Evette said, all the way from the tree to the kitchen entrance...incredible!

As emotionally ill, depressed, and tormented as our father was, who, yes, was also as mean as a snake to the young ones, he bought every single one of those Christmas gifts by working as a mechanic and sometimes a second job as a cab driver for twelve plus hours a day, never less than six days a week. Perhaps Bernie spent some of her money in those later years, as he allowed her to work, but by then we did not get all that stuff, as we were growing up.

As unable as our father was to love his children in the right way, he showed his love at Christmastime under the direction of our mother, whom I am sure said, "I need this much money to get all of our children these gifts." And they did it, year after year. I wonder how stressful it was feeding and clothing seven children and then doing that extra, not just at Christmas, but also the start of school and other special occasions. And then our dad had our stepsister's mother always crying broke. I remember that and I also remember her physically fighting with our mother. But he should have taken care of our other sister, as she was his, along with at least one or possibly two of her brothers, but that is another letter for another time.

So now that I am an adult, I want to say thank you Mom and Dad for all you did, all you sacrificed, how you scrimped and saved and made it happen for us on those special days and, in fact, every day of our lives. I never remember being hungry or cold when our father was alive. I never remember the fridge being empty. I never remember the milk money not being there or not having a salami and cheese sandwich to take for lunch.

We were not always shown love in ways that would have made us more emotionally healthy as adults, but God kept us and for this I am grateful. My sisters, we are all in our older years now with the memories, some bitter and some sweet, but thank the

Lord we are here to continue this journey of healing through remembrance together.

Until we write again...

Peace and Love,
Lil Diva

Hey Divas,

Chitterling cleaning reminds me of happier times and the few times I can remember Big Lind trying to help out with the cooking. I remember Sunday mornings waking up to the sound of Big Lind and Bernie in the kitchen conversing as they smoked Camels and Lucky Strikes while cleaning chitterlings. Bernie would always be moving about, from the boiling pots on the stove, to the table, to the ice box, from getting breakfast for us to preparing dinner, and telling Big Lind not to throw the chitterlings away with the fat scraps.

Walking into the kitchen early on Sunday mornings, I would see Big Lind sitting at one corner of the table, still with his white T-shirt and boxers on, with brown paper bags spread out, cigarette burning and a nip in a drink glass, pulling the fat lumps from the chitterlings, dumping them in a bucket on the floor, and putting the semi-cleaned chitterlings in another pile for the thorough cleaning Evette remembers helping out with.

I hated eating cereal at the same table and smelling them chitterlings and then hurrying off to put on a dress to go to church. I would think the milk tasted like chitterlings, and my whole body smelled like chitterlings, until we left the house and the fresh air seemed to cleanse the smell away.

Although I didn't like the smell of chitterlings, I didn't mind eating the chitterlings with hot sauce. I liked the way they tasted. But I wouldn't eat them without the two side dishes of coleslaw and spaghetti. I used to think we were rich because our mother had a magical way of making meals that matched. She just didn't cook anything for the sake of cooking. Every meal had its side courses to complement the whole meal.

That Cuddly Dudley Christmas I always dubbed as "Kevin's First Christmas." I remember how beautiful the tree was and how there were so many gifts they seemed to fill the whole living room. We barely had room to sit and open the gifts. I remember the little red wagon. That wagon was Kevin's, but also everyone else's in the family. I remember all three of our brothers and Evette being pulled up and down the sidewalk in that wagon, and I remember hustling with that wagon, too. We would pull it up and down the alleys, collecting bottles, and pulling the bottles to Centrella's, where we would cash them in for candy money.

I remember being sick and away from home a lot, too. I remember the playroom at the hospital—it seemed so big, like a child's wonderland! There were so many toys, stuffed animals, books, games, and things to make. I also remember sitting and playing in that playroom. I played with toys and things with our brother, Lil Lind, every day, after the nurses would feed and bathe us. I remember sometimes he would just sit and not play, and I didn't understand that he was sicker than I was at times. I also loved making things for all of you when I was away.

I remember quite a few times how the nurses would send me home with enough stuff to make Valentines and other arts and crafts to share with everyone in the family. When you guys would come home from school, I would be so happy and everyone treated me so nice. I can remember we would sit around the table in the living room and cut and paste and draw whatever I had. I also remember the piano and how Bernie could play jazzy songs by ear and we would all dance around while she played.

I can remember Big Lind and Bernie had grown-up happy times, too. I remember the weekend parties at the house when Aunt Janie, Aunt Prudence, and other folks would gather in the living room and Big Lind would shut the sliding door, and we used to try to peek through the crack in the door. The grownups would drink and dance to kill that roach. Big Lind would pick up the end of the rug and stamp and squish his feet as if he was really killing a roach. And they did a booty dance called "Walkin' the Dog."

I will never forget how our mother told the story of how I and Cousin Lenore woke up after one of them all-night parties and the grownups had left a hidden fifth of liquor behind that green sofa and Lenore and I found it and drank it. When Bernie woke up, she said she thought we had polio or something and took us to the hospital, and that's when she said that Dr. Hill found out I had sickle cell anemia. I was around two years old.

I also remember them having date nights. Big Lind would take Bernie to Riverview Park. I remember a time that they were supposed to go on a date, and Bernie was all dressed and ready to go, and he didn't come home on time, and when he did come home, they argued and Bernie was crying.

I remember how I loved that pink shift dress Bernie wore. The dress was made of really nice material, and it buttoned up the front, with a black-and-white polka-dot lining. One night they both came to visit us at the hospital, and the buttons on her dress were torn. I could tell she had been crying, and she tried to cover up her tears. I remember Big Lind, still smelling of the garage, with his blue work clothes on, sitting on my bed and eating something from the dinner tray, while trying to make me laugh, and he promised me they would not fight anymore.

I also thought if Little Lind and I would get better they would not fight, as this was how I associated the fights. As a child, I did not realize it was not all about me, but today I realize sickness and bills can add stress to any situation. I also remember Big Lind examining bills and working and laying his paycheck on the headboard of their bed or on his tall dresser. Sometimes I would try to peek at the bills and his paycheck. I remember Bernie always saying after Big Lind died, "They can't get blood out of a turnip."

Because of our life experiences of having and not having, and the deeds and tenacity of our parents, this scripture reminds me of these words spoken by our mother: "I am not saying this because I am in need, and I know what it is to have plenty. I have learned the secret of being content in any and every situation, whether well fed or hungry, whether living in plenty or in want. I can do all this through him who gives me strength" (Philippians 4:11–13). Even after Big Lind passed away and we learned as a family to do without, and the struggles we all encountered with addiction, including when Bernie lost the house, wherever she lay her head, we were always welcome to share her space with her. As a grownup now, I can look back and say, "Thank you God for the parents you sent me."

Straight from the heart,
Sadie

Hey Divas,

You would think holidays should be all happy memories. I remember one Christmas that Bernie's boyfriend, Tim, brought all of us bathroom towel sets for Christmas. I was probably around sixteen years-old. I remember how excited I was when I opened that gift, seeing the brightly colored towel set, in a box with tissue paper. I believe we all got different colored sets. He knew that our linen closet wasn't normal, where you could go and get towels. In the end, I am not sure what was even kept in there. He also knew that our bathroom was not a place where you could take a bath, or shower and hang your towel afterwards, as it was more than likely to be blood stained by whoever was shooting up their dope in the bathroom at the time and decided to use it to wipe their arm. I re-call many times not being able to use the bathroom, as it was being occupied by an addict, only to finally enter and see blood splattered on the sink, toilet and tub. It took me years after moving out of that house to be ok with hanging my towel in my bathroom.

With love,
Jewels

CHAPTER 7
Scary and Dangerous Times

"You will not fear the terror of the night, for he will command his angels concerning you to guard you in all your ways."
—Psalm 91:5 and 11

APRIL 2015

Hey Divas,

I remember how Evette would fight my battles for me on the school bus. I was timid, never wanting to fight, nor did I have the energy. Looking back, the Taylor boys and Janice Smith were bullies. One day Evette beat the mess out of Bobbie Taylor on the bus for picking on me.

One night, Bernie sent us to the store to get her cigarettes, and I told Evette to stop throwing the snowballs at the cars, because I was scared she would bust a windshield. It was blinding snow, and cars were sliding all over the road with zero visibility. I could not run, especially with my health and the heavy winter clothes. That last snowball she threw busted the windshield of the snaggle-tooth man who worked at the rug company. He chased Evette, but could not catch her, so he came back and took the end of my hat (we all had long-tailed Santa Claus–shaped hats that winter), and smashed my head into that tree on the corner of Church and Brown as hard as he could. When we got back home, I was crying and bleeding and Bernie cleaned me up and my tooth was broken. I remember having a hard knot on my head and a really bad headache, too. Bernie was more afraid than we were. She told me to tell Big Lind that I had fallen on the snow coming from school because she didn't want him to know she had sent us out in the dark.

Psalm 91 reminds me of good and evil in the world and how God covers us and keeps us. After all the dark alleys and streets I have walked through during my using years, I know that it was nothing but God's saving grace and His angels that kept a watch over me. I always believed in God's angels. I have kept the refrigerator magnet with Psalm 91.11 up since I stopped using.

I recently was faced with revisiting and gaining a deeper meaning of the whole Psalm 91 when I missed the last sister call and asked what the scripture reading was. I was told it was Psalm 91. I do not believe it was a coincidence that my pastor preached from this very same Psalm the following Sunday because I needed the security of the scripture to bring me comfort.

As I was just about to enjoy my birthday week and thinking about how happy I was that I have two new great-nephews and a great-great-nephew, tragic events began to take place in the world again and in our family. With Cousin Lloyd's murder, I began to reflect on past disputes and how when someone was angry they just fought it out. What happened to a good old' fist fight to settle angry emotions? I assumed if people would stop and think, I'm about to take out somebody's father, brother, mother, sister, etc., then the world would be more trusting, like when we grew up and could sleep with the door open so the summer breeze could travel through the whole house. However, there is much more violence in the world today. I never believed in the death penalty because I thought the perpetrator would never have a chance to repent and get to know Jesus. I always believed that God is the only real judge of man.

Prior to the murder of our nephew Lil Floyd and cousin Lloyd, I could not remember anyone in our family passing from a tragic event, but then I started to reflect on Uncle Richard. I loved Uncle Richard. I remember how full of life he was and how he would entertain us and keep a smile on our mother's face. Uncle Richard would take that big, silver, beat-up pot, with the burnt bottom, out of our kitchen cabinet and sit on the front porch or in the living room and play it like a bongo. I used to think that between him beating that pot and it burning on the stove, it would soon see the day when a hole would appear in the bottom of it.

I missed a lot of school when I was younger, and Uncle Richard would always cheer me up when he visited. He would take me to the poolroom and stop at Pop's drug store and buy me candy. I remember the crowds on Church Street and feeling protected by Uncle Richard. I remember the dim lights over the pool tables, the draft of the cold from outside, and sitting in a chair, watching him play pool, with a cigarette always hanging from one side of his mouth.

I also remember how the broken glass counter in the drugstore reminded me of Uncle Richard's tragic demise. I remember how he had more epileptic seizures after that injury and how much pain it caused our mother. I can only imagine that Mama was hurt too since everyone in the community relied on Pop to fill prescriptions. I didn't like old man Pop after that incident.

I thought he was mean and evil, and when I had to go into the drugstore, I would look him straight in the eye, thinking I didn't like him anymore.

However, the first time I began to believe in evil is when Sis said she saw that witch flying out the window when we lived on the West Side of Chicago while our childhood house was being built. To counteract that evil witch that kept me afraid of the dark, I used to love to watch the *Wizard of Oz,* because I began to believe in the Good Witch Glinda and how with a stroke she killed the Wicked Witch of the West. The scripture that reminds me of the unforeseen power of evil is, "We wrestle not against flesh and blood, but powers and principalities in high places" (Ephesians 6:12).

When I reflect back over my life, I realize the power of prayer and how God sends His angels to have charge over us and protect us in all of our ways (Psalm 91:11). I remember when our baby sister told me about how she awoke in that field when she was left for dead, and when she awoke from snow flurries, only a shadow of a figure appeared as she awoke and walked toward home down that dark street. All I could do was say, "Thank you Jesus." I'm not sure if she thought I believed her at that time, but inside all I could do was smile, because I knew God's angels were watching over her and protecting her.

During this period, someone was killing women in Milwaukee, WI, my hometown at that time and leaving them in empty lots, and all I could do was thank God for His saving grace and praise Him for answered prayers. I used to keep Baby Sis on our church prayer list. I remember mourning a young lady I didn't even know. She was not so lucky. She had joined our church on one Sunday, and the next Sunday it was announced that her body was found in an empty lot in the same community. I was sad because I never got a chance to witness her—I never got a chance to get to know her and her story.

Cousin Lloyd has crossed over. He was not so lucky. All I know is that trusting God is what takes me through life's journey, never really knowing or being able to predict anything outside of God's love for humanity. I know God only wants what is best for us and that Psalm 91 is a great testament of God's love and protection for us in the midst of an uncaring world.

Straight from the heart,
Sadie

Hey Divas,

After reading Carolyn's letter, I started thinking about my using years and walking in those dark places and going with anybody just to get high and not even thinking about what could happen to me. It then came to me this overwhelming feeling of how good God is because He took care of me through all of it. It touched me so that Carolyn mentioned the story I told her and that she believed me because I didn't think she did.

Till this day, I remember that night, and after that, I knew it was not enough for me to do God's will, but I also needed to know that something was watching over me and loving me, when I didn't love myself. This brought back so many memories for me just reading Carolyn's story and I had to read Psalm 91, and a great story it is. I'm truly overwhelmed now and at a loss for words, so I'm going to pray that God's word continues to work on me.

Love,
Ms. Evette

Diva Five Alive

Hey Divas,

I never knew Uncle Richard was missing an eye, or I don't remember, but as I type, I believe I can see the patch. I do think I remember him being really tall. I never knew the story about how he lost his eye, and I am confused about the broken glass at the drugstore and how that related to the loss of his eye and his death.

When Carolyn talked about Uncle Richard beating the pot, I could almost see and hear him, but I have no memories of that either. I feel so blessed that Carolyn was able to be taken care of during her sickness by Uncle Richard, who made her feel special and protected. However, her tradeoff for that was great because of how sick she was and how much pain she was always in. It is such a miracle that she survived, and how blessed she is to have natural intelligence, because she did miss a lot of school, but that has not affected her ability to learn and to become the educated woman she is today.

What I do remember about Richard is the time he had an epileptic seizure (or fit, as they called it back then) at the house. I was the only one home with Bernie at the time. (Perhaps I was home sick, because with all of those kids, how was that ever possible to be home alone with her?) I do remember it was during the daytime and Bernie grabbed me and took me to hide behind the bedroom door of the boys' room. I remember her being so scared, and because of that, I was afraid, as well. I remember her telling me to be really quiet as we crouched down behind that door for what seemed like hours. I remember hearing the noise of the kitchen chairs and table, as Uncle Richard had probably fallen down during his seizure and was knocking things around. I don't remember anything else after that.

As I type this, I am so grateful for Bernie and how I felt protected by her during that time. I miss her. I thought Uncle Richard died from having a seizure outside in the winter and that he was found frozen to death. At least, that is the story I remember.

But what I do remember is that I didn't like Pop that much either. He was kind of creepy. I didn't mind him calling me Lil Macklin though, because it made me feel special that our family name was known. I do remember the lady who worked in his store for years; I believe her name was Eunice. She was a nice lady. I think she had buckteeth and was not very attractive and wore one of those big puffy hairdos.

I remember one time I bought a candy bar from "Pop's" and I was so excited, only to bite down and discover it was full of worms. I was so grossed out, and I remember how it took all of the courage I had to take it back and ask for my money back. This makes me think about how I have always had a problem asking for what I want or talking about when I have felt wronged, but praise God I have gotten better at that!

Eunice was so nice to me. She apologized and gave me my money back and said the worms probably came because it was so hot outside. I do remember in the latter years how Pop would sell Robitussin to the adults without a prescription because they would drink it and get high. I lost all respect for him once I found out about that.

I also remember the story of the flying witch, and as I think of it now, it brings a smile to my face, thinking of the bad witch in *The Wizard of Oz*. LOL, I don't know how much I believe the story of the flying witch, but hey, anything is possible, and our memories are our memories, each being unique.

I too am so grateful that God spared me from horrible things, such as being assaulted, raped, or catching a felony (as I picked up a cocaine drop and delivered it from the airport to a hotel one time, and I also sold drugs), or even killed. I can remember walking through dark alleys by myself at all times of the night just to cop that bag of cocaine. I must have been out of my mind because today I am scared of my own shadow and don't know how I had the nerve to do that. I am so grateful that God delivered me from drug addiction, and I am not foolish enough to believe that I can ever "sample" it again. In fact, one day not that long ago, I thought about snorting cocaine, and I could actually experience it, as I recalled that high, and it scared me to death. I never, ever, want to be in the presence of that drug, or any drug, for that matter.

When I think about it, all of us Gibert/McBride sisters are very courageous and have taken many chances in our lives. God has been so merciful and kind in keeping us safe. I remember several times riding into the night on the North Side of Chicago and walking into unknown places (sometimes through alleys) to purchase my cocaine, but I never once was assaulted. I also know that we are very blessed to not have been raped by the many men who frequented our house in those days.

I do remember one of Bernie's friends, named "Toothy," I think, though I can't remember his real name. I was about seventeen at the time and he had children my age and I believe older. One time he drove me to his house so that we could "get high." He told me that other people were going to be there. He gave me a Quaalude, which I promptly swallowed, because I would take anything, pill, or snort, or whatever (even heroin, though just a few times), to get high and escape the reality of my world. That was my very first time taking a Quaalude. Anyway, I remember feeling too high and so I asked him to take me home, which he did. He certainly could have raped me, but I believe he had more sense than to do that, but I am sure he was hoping if I got high enough, I would just "give it up." Disgusting old geezer!

I do believe, because of the incest, having sex did not come easy for me, for which I am grateful, because I never traded sex for drugs. I would always proudly say I always bought my dope because I always had a job. I was a working cocaine/free-base addict. Yes, there were plenty of times I pawned everything in my house and even one time my car, but I would always get it back on payday, and boy did I always live paycheck to paycheck.

Thank you for the light of Jesus that led and guided Evette during that near-death experience. I remember she told me that when she "came to" she was in a field or a parking lot and did not know where she was. She said that a man appeared, who I now know was an angel, and told her to walk toward the light, and that is what led her out of that dark place, where that man had left her for dead. She said once the man told her to walk toward the light, he disappeared. I know he was an angel. Thank God for his son who continues to light our paths in this dark, dark world!

With love,
Jewels

Divas,

I remember the quarter parties and how we negotiated with the Fuller boys not to have them at the same time. I think they started the quarter parties, but we quickly took over to first place. It was my Sweet Sixteen party where there was a D.J. I think Marilyn's boyfriend had found. I wore a yellow body-hugging sweater dress with poofs from the waist on down. I can see it now, the strobe lights going, the music rocking, and everybody who was anybody was there.

That was the day I drank something and was drugged, because I went on a trip that lasted well into the next day. I did not know I was being drugged, nor do I know who did it. It took me a while

Diva Five Alive

to realize I was on a trip. But every color was brighter, things were moving faster, then slower. It was like watching a movie and I was in it. I watched people's mouths move and no sounds came out. And my feet were not touching the ground.

Coming down from that trip, I remember being in the backyard in the morning looking at some bug on a blade of grass. Everything was magnified. My final thought on that infamous first trip had to do with seeing Terrance standing across the street waiting for the Number 8 bus, and it was way too early for it to come. I think he might have been the one who slipped the Mickey into my Kool-Aid, and it was Kool-Aid, because I had sworn I would never drink alcohol.

There would be more trips to come of my own accord and a devastating addiction that lasted two decades. That was a short-lived "Sweet Sixteen" in more ways than one. And finally gone are the days of the body to be envied, but I do remember the blue three-piece suit, and if I must say so myself, I did look good.

Until next time...

Peace and Love,
Lil Diva

Divas,

How sad for any woman to carry a child full-term and not be able to bring her baby home to grow and live. My first memory of our lost sister surfaced when I use to ride from Wisconsin to Illinois to visit Sunset Cemetery with my girlfriend who also lost her little girl in the late 1980s. Her baby also died several days after birth, but she had a name, and she had a burial, and she has her own little lot in the special baby's section at Sunset Gardens. I wish

I knew what the rules and/or laws were in the sixties versus the eighties. Why didn't our sister have a gravesite or a burial? Did she have a name? Did she even have a birth certificate?

My memory of our mother lying at the bottom of the stairs in the basement being pregnant was first triggered by one of our visits to Sunset to memorialize our loved ones. I'm not sure if she fell down the stairs or if she was pushed during a fight with our father. I'm not sure if this is a memory I witnessed or a story I was told, but my mind comes back to this same image of her lying at the bottom of the stairs whenever I think about our missing sister.

I remember the pain in her side she suffered during this pregnancy after the fall, and I remember how beautiful she looked pregnant, and how the glow of motherhood outshined any emotional or physical abuse she suffered. What a warrior she was, what a trouper. She kept on having babies, while mothering and nurturing us, no matter what personal abuses she suffered.

I remember our mother going to deliver the baby girl, but she came back home without our sister. She said the baby girl was beautiful but lived for only nine days. I wondered why she did not have a funeral or a burial like my girlfriend's baby girl. What did they do with babies that died after birth in the sixties? I wonder what name was picked out for her. If my memory is correct, the baby girl was between Michael and Kevin, so we did have a younger baby sister, for real! I wonder how she would look today, who she took after most.

I used to think our sister, Lynn, was just a relative who looked like our father, until I got older, but this thought faded with age and memories of her birth mother, Ms. G. The last time I remember Lynn visiting was when she snatched dad's wallet while he was drunk sleeping and he chased her through the alley in his boxers barefoot. I never remember much else about her except she had to go away to get well. I remember thinking, how can she be born the same year as Brenda if she was our sister, and if she is our sister, who is the oldest?

As a child, I don't know if Lynn told me this or if I witnessed it myself, but I have a memory of her mother tying her to her bed, both feet and both legs. When entering their house, you walked right into the front room, and the bedroom off to the right is where Lynn lay tied to the bed. When I walked into the house, her mother told me to wait at the door. The door to the bedroom to the right of the entrance was open a crack, and I saw Lynn tied to the bed. Before I left that day, I remember her mom telling me she couldn't come over to our house.

Why was I at their house? I don't know, but I've had this memory all of my life. The last time this memory surfaced was when Lil Diva texted and said Lynn's mom had passed away. In fact, I didn't know I still had memories of her until that day I found out she had passed away. When I heard this news, I was not sad, I was angry, because I had always harbored bad memories of her, and I never liked her.

Another bad memory I had of her was when she started a fight with our mother in our front yard. She had walked over to our house, and I remember our dad was in the middle, and she was at the front door and was trying to swing at our mom around our dad, and somehow the fight pursued to the front yard, and one of the big, white, wooden poles that anchored the front porch fell on the front lawn. I remember screaming and kicking at her because our mother was lying in the grass under that pole, and I thought she was hurt really bad.

As these memories surfaced about our sister, Lynn, and her mom, I realized I had to ask God for forgiveness and to remove the unforgiving spirit from my heart. Since then, I have discovered that Lynn is still alive and living in Elgin, Illinois. Now, as an adult myself, I realize as a child that everything and everyone that causes harm to your parent(s) is traumatic.

Rest in peace, Mom, for you are a real trouper. Rest in peace, Dad, for you were a great provider. Rest in peace, Ms. G. Lord, keep Lynn and send your angels to have charge over her life and keep her in all her ways, and bless her, too!

Straight from the heart,
Sadie

Julie, Brenda, Carolyn and Kevin

CHAPTER 8
Fun Times

"How great is his joy in the victories you give!"
—Psalm 22:1

FAMILY VACATIONS
DECEMBER 2017

Hey Divas,

In our family, vacation was not a part of our growing up. It was a luxury that we, like many other families in our community, could not afford. The summer zoo and amusement park trips were wonderful and memorable experiences and as close to a "vacation" as we would come. There were also the picnics at the Forest Preserves that we looked forward to, because there was nothing like unpacking delicious fried chicken and potato salad from the cooler, which was prepared by our Bernie. The special treat of canned soda pop and ice-cold watermelon made our mouths water. After eating, we would run off those calories galloping through the woods on our "adventures."

The best vacation of all was our family fishing trip taken in a motor home that was attached to my father's car. Family, at this point, was my mom, dad, and sisters. Extended family on this particular trip included our aunt (my mother's sister) and our good neighbor who lived next door. Before we left to drive to a fishing spot in Illinois, my father would park the motor home on the side of the house and everyone in the neighborhood got a tour. My goodness, did that make me feel special! I remember kids saying, "You all must have a lot of money." I have no idea how this motor home was acquired, but as I reflect, I believe it was

Bernie and Nicole

probably loaned to us by our father's boss at the mechanic shop. Their generosity and love for our family had been shown in times past in other ways, as well. In any case, we were so excited about the trip that I remember not being able to sleep as we prepared to get on the road while it was still dark. We all rode in the motor home (trailer) while my father and the neighbor drove until we reached our destination. My mom may have also taken the wheel at some point.

Inside the motor home, I remember the eating table folded up and that area became sleeping space. There was also a bunk over the stove where my aunt slept. One night, as she climbed in the bunk, her foot inadvertently turned the gas range on. I remember it clearly because my mother, who had a keen sense of smell, detected the odor, and it was turned off. I specifically remember my mom saying that we could have all died!

The hours my mom and aunt spent fishing were serious times. They sat for hours fishing with the worms we caught the night before in the backyard and that stinky dough-bait my mother made out of cornmeal and other ingredients. I remember getting a chance to cast the pole and hold it until there was a bite. But I found it to be quite boring, as it took so long and you had to be quiet. Big Lind did more drinking than fishing, and as with most outings, he ended up laid out intoxicated on the ground, sleeping it off.

The time we spent while the adults fished were similar to the adventures we had during the Forest Preserve outings: running through the vast wooded areas, playing spontaneous games, and getting scrapes, cuts, and various bug bites. I can still taste that nasty water from the pumps on the grounds, which you had to drink if you were thirsty. We had the same great picnic food, along with sandwiches and other stuff, to last us for the short trip, which seemed like a wonderful eternity.

Diva Five Alive

My greatest memory was the visit of the bear at the trailer. In the middle of the night, we heard a loud knocking on the door, and I distinctly remember seeing a large dark form in the trailer window and Bernie saying, "It's a bear—be quiet." I don't recall being afraid, because children can be fearless, but it was more like, Wow—this is a real adventure and will I ever have a story to tell!

I don't know what happened that caused Mr. Bear to leave, but he left and did not kill my father and our neighbor as they slept in the car. I remember that was a vocalized fear, just like the fear I expressed when I thought we could have been killed by the gas. My goodness, more drama for the story!

Being so long ago, my memories are not crystal-clear, but the feeling is still alive in me as I write, as these were, strangely enough, the good old days!

Peace and Love,
Lil Diva

PIANO RECITALS

Divas,

Initially, when I was thinking about what I would write about for my "Fun Times" story, I thought of Fourth of July holidays, as that was a time when we would get new red, white, and blue outfits. I remember a particular Fourth of July when Big Diva had on this smokin' hot red, white, and blue hot pants outfit, which she wore with gladiator sandals and her very large afro. I also remember how shapely she was, Brenda too, which I was somewhat envious of, because I had no butt, giant breasts, and a little pug in the tummy area. Big Diva and Brenda were what you would call

Marilyn "Big Diva"

"stacked" back in the day. I also thought they looked good in whatever clothes they wore.

I also thought about how we loved to dance and would have dance contests at the house. I remember how we would dance in the front yard, and one time a man driving by was so caught up looking at us he had an accident. Thank God no one was hurt, and it was probably not funny, but I remember laughing anyway. Big Diva has always been and continues to be a good dancer. Me, I don't have much coordination when it comes to dancing, but I still love to move to music.

When I began to think about our love for music, I thought about the piano recitals we used to have. Now there were a lot of things I did not like about the process building up to the piano recitals. One part I particularly did not like was walking to the piano teacher's home. I have always had a fear of being attacked by a dog, and whenever I would walk alone and hear dogs bark, I would get really scared. I also remember having to walk by the house of this old man who was rumored to have killed his wife with a hammer. Now, how true that is, I really don't know. Even though I never once saw the old man, just walking past his house invoked fear in me.

Then it was the piano lessons. Ms. Bentley was the teacher. She was an old mean lady who would hit my hands with her ruler whenever I made a mistake. She also had a collection of scary-looking porcelain dolls, and I used to think about how mad she would probably get if I accidently broke one. She had them sitting on her sofa, and I believe some were on top of the piano, as well. They had eyes that opened and closed that seemed to watch my every move, and their mouths appeared to be smiling, as if they were laughing at me.

Needless to say, piano lesson time was not a good memory. However, the recitals were all worth it. Even though I was painfully shy and had stage fright, I loved the recitals. I loved dressing up in pretty, crisp, clean, white dresses and wearing pretty headbands. I felt like a princess and I loved that feeling. I also loved the unconditional support of the audience. I am sure none of us played like Beethoven, but the audience was always supportive and provided praise and applause. I remember one particular recital when Bernie played a duet with someone. I recall her pretty legs and how I thought she looked so beautiful.

Even though Bernie never took formal piano lessons, she was musically gifted and could play music by ear and had the gift of making up her own songs. At home she would sit at the piano and play what us kids called "boogie woogie music." We would all gather around in the living room and dance to the music she played. Music has a way of transporting you to a different time and space. Maybe that's why we loved it so much, as it was always a way to leave the space we were in.

With Love,
Jewels

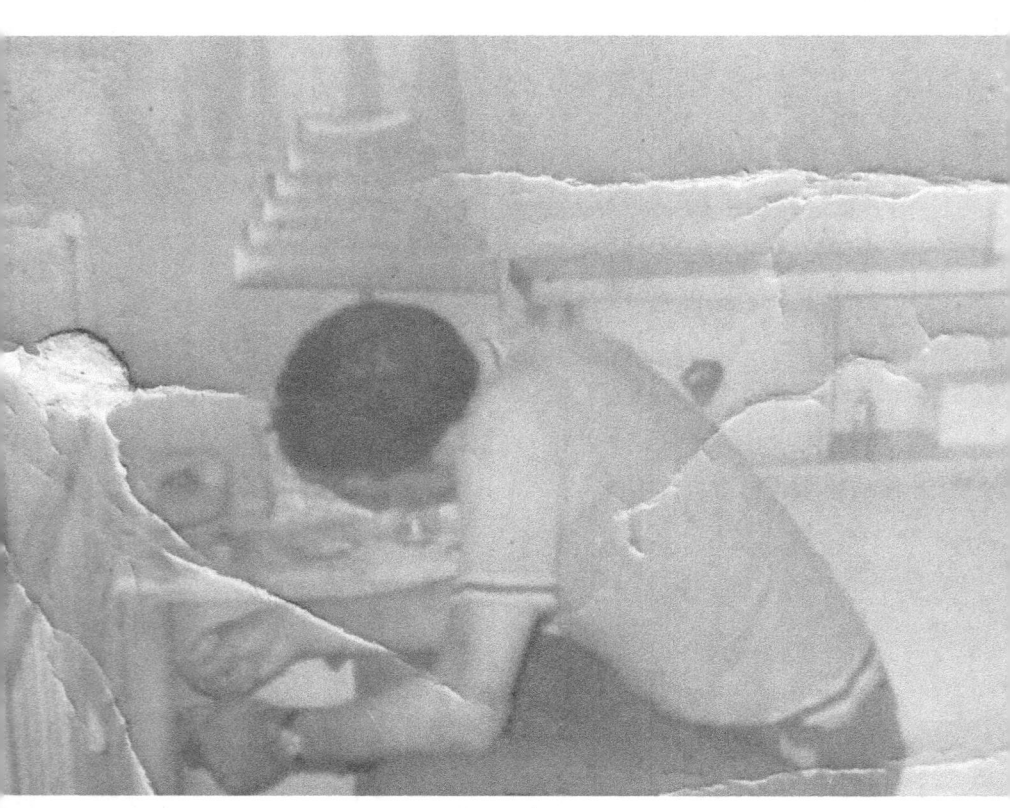
Big Lind

CHAPTER 9
Mental Illness

"It was good for me to be afflicted so that I might learn your decrees."
—Psalm 119:71

JULY 2014

Divas,

July is National Minority Mental Health Month. When I thought about this, I thought about how our family has been impacted by mental illness.

I wondered what our grandfather, who went to the garage and shot himself to death one day, would have been diagnosed with. I wonder what his demons were. I think about my grandmother, who encouraged my father, when he had my mother pinned to the floor during one of their many fights, but this time he had a shotgun to her head and my grandmother was saying, "Shoot that bitch." Who but a "crazy" woman would encourage her son to murder his wife in front of his kids?

I think about our stepsister, Lynn, and how her mental illness has kept her in a psychiatric hospital for all of her adult life.

I think about Bernie and how when her depression hit, she painted her room a dark purple and put up black curtains, which she often kept drawn, as she lay in bed for days, only to emerge when drugs were being offered. I remember her receiving the diagnosis of schizophrenia and how she said she saw Jesus talking to the disciples in the picture of the Last Supper that hung on our kitchen wall. I remember her multiple hospitalizations at Reed Mental Hospital and how she would get her shots of Thorazine and then get sent home. I remember visiting her a few times and being confused and not being sure what to say.

I remember the first time, and only time, I smelled her body odor when she was on the front porch one day. This is a poignant memory because she was so clean and loved to bathe and wear her perfumes. I remember thinking, what could possibly be wrong with her, having decided not to bathe?

I remember the time she got a suitcase and ran out of the house in her house robe, that light-purple one, with the stitching. She said she was going to go see Ted. I remember trying to stop her and she pushed me back with what seemed like super-human strength coming from a woman. The ambulance was called that night and she was again taken to Reed's. I remember how she walked down the middle of Church Street stark-naked and how embarrassing that was. I guess she would probably be what we call "dual diagnosis" today, as she was also using drugs. What came first, the drugs or the mental illness? And does it really matter?

I think about how Kevin said he was told, I believe in prison, that he is bipolar. I think about how Naomi has that same diagnosis.

I think about how menopause, a sudden breakup, a change in my living situation, and countless other things have set off the dormant depression in me, which I am sure lies in all of us. I think about how sometimes it is so severe and smoldering within me, I feel like I want to scream, but not really knowing where the scream is coming from.

I think about how I have thought at times that death would be a welcome relief, but I would never go that route because of all the love that surrounds me in my children and my family. However, most of all, I think about how gracious God is, and even in the midst of it all, how He keeps us.

I am reminded of the scripture that a speaker from Kenya preached from James 5:17: "Elijah was a man just like us." He said, "Elijah struggled with fear, rejection, self-pity, depression, suicidal tendencies, and being broke." He went on to say, "Elijah was a great man of faith; he was just like us." With that being said, even though this month brings attention to mental illness, I am also reminded that I am more than a conqueror through Him, and that He loves me and I will continue to do all I can to erase the stigma of mental illness.

Those are my thoughts.

With love,
Jewels

Hey Divas,

When I reflect on our mother's mental illness, I have a sea of thoughts about it. But instead of revisiting those memories, I thought of the reason I chose to do my college major in Mental Health with a focus on Addiction. It was because I wanted to learn about our family diseases, addiction and mental illness, which often go hand in hand.

While I was in school, I made a drastic career change, which I now know was preparation for ministry, and I went into the field of social services to become a drug counselor, so I could help other people overcome their addictions, God having given me the direction and the grace to do this.

Ironically, because I became a good AODA (Alcohol and Other Drug Abuse) counselor and was naturally compassionate, my supervisor always assigned me the MISA (Mentally Ill Substance Abuser) clients. This was before the state licensing agency began to require a specific certification to serve this population. Everyone on the unit knew I would get the "special people."

I loved my clients and they loved me. I cried with them and for them, as we tried to get to the root of the reason for their addiction. And sometimes it was just too difficult because many were so deep into the mental illness that they were beyond deciphering what had happened in their lives. I was never shocked by the client's behavior, and believe me, some of them clowned out. However, I was never afraid of them or that they would hurt me, and I know it was because of what I experienced with our mother as a child and then as a young adult.

I began to understand the difference between when Bernie was really sick and when she was seeking attention. And now that I am saved and understand that demons are real, I know now that I was often in the presence of legions. I remember her voice changing and the evil eyes that did not belong to my mother. But I also remember that I was rarely afraid and something inside me, which I now know was God, bore witness to my spirit and let me know that love was stronger than that sickness. I knew I should try not to be mad, ashamed, or embarrassed, but be strong and try to gain some understanding of the pattern of our mother's episodes. I remember focusing on staying calm with her, telling her I loved her and she was going to be all right. Sometimes she would just cry, and other times the demon would smirk at me.

I remember feeling like something was wrong with me because I was not embarrassed about her walking out stark-naked in broad daylight. I felt sad and oddly numb, but now I believe God was just strengthening me, because there would be much more I had to handle in years to come—the trips to the mental hospital, the medication, me a child trying to talk to doctors who thought they could just brush me off because I was young.

Through discernment, I realized that whatever she had, which I believe was paranoid schizophrenia, was a seasonal disorder. When the seasons changed, like clockwork, I could count on there being a buildup and then a blowout. Sometimes she would come out of it on her own, and many times she would not, and the hospital, medication, and family disruption cycle would begin all over again.

I remember once talking to Mama about Bernie and she said, "I don't know what's wrong with her and I can't do anything about it." I recall being upset at her response, but now I know she prayed, which may have been the reason our mother did not kill herself or somebody else. Aunt Lula would ask, "What the hell is wrong with her?" Or she would say "she is crazy," as it made her so nervous. She could not be around that, and I remember her crying about it one time, as it had to hurt to see her sister like that. I recall feeling so helpless and wishing there was an adult I could turn to for help, but there was none—I was the adult.

So, we can add one more word to the description of our mother—she was a survivor, and so are we, of addiction and emotional/mental illness, diagnosed or not. We are still here to tell the story, and I have my own stories of multiple suicide attempts and craziness in my head. I still fight depression and anxiety and have to always watch for my addictive tendencies to manifest in other areas of my life.

I remember someone once said, "Addiction is suicide on the installment plan." So, with that I will end and thank God that drugs and mental illness did not kill our mother and that I am not making payments on the installment plan anymore. Thank you Jesus!

Life to be continued...

Peace and Love,
Lil Diva

CHAPTER 10
Big Lind

> "To everything there is a season, and a time to every purpose under heaven: a time to weep, and a time to laugh; a time to mourn, and a time to dance..."
> —ECCLESIASTES 3:1–4

JANUARY 2015

Hey Divas,

It's funny how when you miss someone and think about the good memories, suddenly you feel as if you are reliving the exact moment or experience. Sometimes I miss Bernie so much, but this past holiday season it was Big Lind who I missed immensely. I thought about him all during the holiday season and beyond.

The murder of our nephew and a conversation with Cousin Tona made me realize how much I yearned to see our father. Cousin Tona was trying to arrange for her or Joseph to come out to Evanston to represent their family at the funeral, and she said,

Diva Five Alive

Bernie and Big Lind

"I don't want to leave Dad alone," and I found myself replying, "No, you should not leave him." I never thought that this simple conversation would make me so sad.

Afterwards, I thought about our father. What would he be like? Would he be sickly from years of alcohol abuse? Would he be sober today? Would he still ask me to make his oyster soup? I found myself not wanting to celebrate anyone else's father, not wanting to call Uncle J.T. and wish him a happy birthday, not wanting to talk to Aunt Johnnie—I just wanted to have a conversation with my own father.

As I thought about him more, I reflected on a time that Jocelyn and I were getting a pedicure together. As my manicurist began to scrub the bottom and sides of my feet, I cringed and laughed, and pulled away. And Jocelyn did the same thing at the same time. Like mother, like daughter, I thought, we are both ticklish when it comes to our feet. Then I remember how Big Lind used to tickle me on the bottom of my feet, making me laugh until it hurt. I remember him turning me upside down on or near that green sofa in the living room and me saying, "No Daddy, no! That's enough!"

And I thought, what a good time I had with my father, and for a moment, I couldn't remember anything bad about him. I just missed him. I thought about how it would be if our children were able to interact with their grandparents, how it would be to have living parents, and how people are lucky to have relationships with their living parents, and I got sad and I felt cheated and alone.

Recently, another incident jolted his presence into my memory, and I had to laugh out loud. I never like peeing in close proximity out in public, and I always close the door when I have company in my house, because I have to admit it does sound loud. I was in our agent's trailer last Sunday, and I had to use the bathroom, and when she walked past the closed bathroom door, I immediately remembered how Big Lind would tease me, asking Bernie if she was sure I didn't have a "ding-a-ling as long as his." I also remember on the weekend, when Bernie would be at the stove, cooking, and Big Lind would be sitting around the kitchen table with his drinking buddies, drinking and snacking and having his grown-up time. When I would walk through the kitchen to use the bathroom, he would have them standing outside the bathroom door listening to me pee, and they all would be laughing, while he would be telling them that I peed louder than a man.

These memories come back to my mind like a great flood when I least expect them to. It's funny how experiences in life can spark a memory that you'd never think about until some simple occurrence jolts the mind. Well, it is springtime now, and I still

Diva Five Alive

miss our parents, but me and Big Lind have had many laughs over the past few months.

Straight from the heart,
Sadie

Hey Divas,

I don't know, call me a cold, unsentimental person, I am not sure, but when I read Carolyn's letter, I thought about how I never think about Big Lind. I never miss him or wonder what he would look like or be like. I don't have any fond memories of him, and it seems unfortunate that the only time he seemed to enjoy us, or to have fun with us, was when he was drunk.

I did chuckle to myself when I read Carolyn's memories of him. I half laughed when she mentioned how he had his friends outside the bathroom as she peed. The half laugh was because I could see a bunch of silly drunk men laughing at that. The half that did not think it was funny probably remembered the sexual abuse I endured from him and how having drunk men outside the bathroom door of your female child was probably not the appropriate thing to have going on. It was also not appropriate for him to mention Carolyn having "a ding-a-ling" to Bernie, as that is not something a young girl should hear.

When Carolyn mentioned the tickling of her feet, I could see her laughing and that brought joy to my heart, but it also made me mad because when you are tickled, you are at the mercy of the person doing the tickling, and even though it makes you laugh, you still want it to stop. That's weird when you think about it. How can something that makes you laugh cause you some kind of discomfort? I guess that's life.

Big Lind

I do remember the time Big Lind put his huge hands around my neck and choked me on that same green sofa. I was gasping for air, thinking I was going to die and how Bernie and my siblings were in the same room and nobody came to help me. I don't know how long the choking went on, but I do remember flailing my arms and legs, having difficulty breathing, and wishing it would stop. I am sure my siblings did not realize what he was doing. I vaguely remember them being in the corner of the living room with Bernie and it seemed as if they were preoccupied with something.

Anyway, I remember going to the bathroom and looking in the mirror after that choking incident and noticing that my face was full of red spots. I know now that they were broken blood vessels from him choking me so hard. Just to think I could have died at the hands of a drunken man who thought choking me was funny.

I hold no bitterness, as I have forgiven him a long time ago, but I would be lying if I said I hold fond memories of him. I guess I stopped looking at him as a father after he stepped into my top bunk that night. I say "stepped," because he was so tall I believe he was able to do just that without needing the ladder, or he probably just used the bottom bunk as a stair. Not that I remember seeing him actually step into my bunk, but what I do remember is being awakened with what I know now was his hard penis pressing against my vagina. Once he realized it was not going to fit, he left my bed and I could hear him go into the refrigerator. He returned and I could smell butter, which I guess he put on his penis to use as a lubricant. I remember lying so still and being so afraid and still his penis did not fit and thank God he did not try to force it. He left my bed that night and whispered to me, "Don't tell your momma." I remember feeling so ashamed the next day and many days after.

This left me with years of shame and I kept the "secret" for years. I did not tell anyone, until I told my aunt, upon her inquiry years after my father died. Even then, I did not tell her the whole story, which was fine because I could tell she did not want to know. I was an adult by then. I then told Brenda about it years later.

I never think about what he would have been like, and I was surprised to realize that had he lived, he would be eighty-one years old. I have forgiven him for what he did to me, although he did something to me that is unthinkable for a man to do to his child. My memories of him are sad ones, with the saddest one being him in his bedroom with empty pints of liquor in the baby crib, which was still in the room, asking me to "call your momma for me." Bernie had left him by then and he was in a depressed and always drunken state. That makes me sad.

I do miss and admire the strength of my mother and feel sad to know she endured so many years married to an abusive alcoholic and how trapped she must have felt. I admire her strength in deciding she wasn't going to take it anymore and having the courage to leave him. I am thankful her strength was passed down to us.

With love,
Jewels

CHAPTER 11
Lil Lind

"Weeping may endure for a night, but joy comes in the morning."
—Psalm 30:5

APRIL 2015

Hey Divas,

The last time when I wrote, mentioning about how hard it must have been for our parents to provide for seven children in the home, after I sent the letter, I remembered there were eight children between our parents, and I made myself a note to write about Lil Lind. Our brothers (living now) did not know their oldest brother. My letter was due yesterday, but I am late, and today is April 1st, April Fools' Day, which was taboo in our house, because that was the day Lil Lind died. I believe I was seven and he was four.

I remember the day vividly. I can see my father comforting my mother as she wept in their bedroom. They did not see or hear me, the bedroom door was cracked, and I could see my dad at the foot of the bed and hear my mother's wail. It was not the cry of a domestic fight, and it was too early for that anyway.

I can see him patting her on the knees and shaking his head, and I could not imagine what was wrong. Things had been hard I know because Carolyn and Lil Lind had just come home from the hospital again. This time they were both in at the same time and came home together. Carolyn seemed better, though so thin and frail, but Lil Lind did not seem well at all.

I have more memories of him being carried than I do of him walking. I remember my dad carrying him in the house when they got back from the hospital, and I remember my mom carrying him to bed the night before, as he did not feel good, he was not talking, and he whined a lot. Now I know it was the pain of the sickle cell disease.

Lil Lind

While my mother cried, I thought I should go in the room and check on him, so I tiptoed in there and went to his bedside. My memories of what happened inside that room after all these years have grown fainter, but as I think back on it now, I believe I was somewhat traumatized and no one ever knew.

I remember touching Lil Lind to wake him and he was so cold, and his body seemed hard, and I kept tapping him, saying, "Wake up, Lil Lind, wake up." He was lying on his back, and the color of his face was dark—I remember a purplish hue. And I remember a smell, and I thought he probably did wet the bed, but it smelled worse than that. That's all I remember, as I think I fainted after that.

I don't remember anybody talking to me or going to my mother or father. I just remember everything went dark. And the darkness lasted a real long time. So many people came to the house and everybody wore dark clothes, everybody was sad and crying, some even harder than our mom, especially her sister, Aunt Prudence. I remember our mother sitting in the corner chair in the living room, blankly staring into space. It seemed like she never went to sleep or did anything but just sit in that chair and cry. I remember the day she wore all-black clothes—it was probably the day of the funeral.

I recall a discussion about whether or not we should go to the funeral and it was decided no, that we were "too little." All I remember is that there were too many people in what seemed like our too little house all the time and there was a whole bunch of food that nobody was eating and our mom was still sitting in that chair.

I don't remember much about our father then, except for the time I saw him bent down in those blue khakis on his knees next my mom who was sitting in that living room chair as she cried and he just shook his head.

Diva Five Alive

The pain, the pain... Now that we have experienced the death of loved ones in our adult lives, we can understand deep grief, but the death of a child, who knows that? I believe it is the number-one cause of stress and depression.

It just makes me realize again how strong our mother had to be, as well as our father, for that matter. That was his oldest son, his namesake, and he would never be able to teach him how to mow grass, fish, drive, polish his shoes, fix cars, drink beer, or whatever. Nor would he be able to see his son marry and give him grandchildren. As the saying goes, only God knows what they really went through.

It eventually got "lighter" in the house. It just seemed like the sun stopped shining for so long. It also seemed like I went away somewhere, but I don't think I did. I believe I was just away in my own childhood pain and grief, and nobody ever talked to me about it in much depth.

I do remember thinking about heaven, which I had heard about in Sunday school, and I believed in it because where else could my little brother have gone?

I still don't recognize April Fools' Day or participate in April Fools' pranks and I never will. Every April 1st, it's not April Fools' Day, but my little brother's heaven birthday, and it always will be, for me.

I love you, Lil Lind, sweet little brother of mine. See you later.

Peace and Love,
Lil Diva

Lil Lind

Hey Divas,

As I read Brenda's letter and her account of Lil Lind's death, I began to think about Big Lind's funeral and how Kevin was looking into the casket and saying, "Wake up, Daddy, wake up." This is the same thing Brenda was saying to Lil Lind: "Wake up." I never knew that story, and it breaks my heart to know that Brenda experienced that and that it was never talked about. Even though I don't have any memories other than what was implanted in my brain from conversations about his death, I still honor my brother's going home day by not playing jokes on April Fools' Day.

One memory or implanted thought that does come to mind has to do with something about Lil Lind's belongings, clothes or something. I remember seeing Big Lind carrying Lil Lind's belongings down the back stairs. I believe there were two concrete stairs leading down to the ground. Perhaps it was the clothes he soiled when he passed away. I am sure the odor Brenda smelled was the release of his bodily fluids, which happens sometimes when people die.

As Brenda said, who knows the death of a child? I hope that I never do. I can't imagine what our mother experienced losing her first son. Just the thought of it makes my heart heavy. I also think about how, even though Big Lind was callous in his ways, he comforted her, and how Brenda remembers seeing him in his blue khakis kneeling at our mom's side. I am sure he had probably dressed for work and was planning on going until he discovered that Lil Lind was dead.

To hear about the compassionate side of my father makes me glad and sad at the same time. The sadness comes from knowing that he experienced the pain of losing his first son and how he had to comfort Bernie and experience his own pain at the same time. I wonder if that is why he never connected with Floyd, Michael, and

Kevin. Was he afraid he would lose them too, or was he resentful because he had lost his firstborn son, his namesake?

When I read that Aunt Prudence cried the hardest, I couldn't help wondering if she was drunk—LOL. I remember when Kevin was born and he was so little and Aunt Prudence came over to see him and almost sat on him because Bernie had placed him on a pillow in a chair.

What dark days those must have been for our parents, especially our mom. She was a strong woman, having fought a lot of battles all by herself. While this is admirable, it is not fair. Sometimes lately I get taken aback when people tell me I am a strong woman. Sometimes I don't want to have to be strong—I just want somebody to help me carry the load. Anyway, we will all see our brother, mother, and father in heaven one day. What a glorious day that will be!

With love,
Jewels

Hey Brenda,

I didn't know Lil Lind either. From our family picture, I saw that I appeared to be between four to six months old, so when reading your letter, I was thinking it must have been so hard on Bernie to take care of an infant (me) and tending to a sick child, well, two, because Carolyn was sick, too. I was wondering where I was in all the darkness you talked about. Of course, I don't know, as I was too young to remember. I can only imagine what you went through at such an early age.

I am so glad you shared that story because it made me realize how strong Bernie had to be going through the loss of a child and

Lil Lind

still being a mother to the rest of her children. I just want to say, Lil Lind, Big Lind, and Bernie, I am so sorry ya'll went through that pain, and may you continue to rest in peace. I love you all, and when my day comes, I will see you then.

Love,
Ms. Evette

Evette, Brenda, Carolyn, Lil Lind and Julie

Marilyn

CHAPTER 12
Wrapping It Up

"The end of a matter is better than its beginning and patience is better than pride."

—Ecclesiastes 7:8

OCTOBER 2013

Hey Divas,

I remember watching our house being built as a little girl from a big hole in the ground to a complete house where we could go downstairs because the whole thing belonged to us. I was so proud to know that our father had that house built from the ground for us, for his family. Our parents were the youngest couple in Evanston during that time period to accomplish that goal of home ownership at such a young age.

Today, I choose to remember the good things, how much in love our parents really were and the good times we had. As a woman today, I have learned a lot through observation. I have learned how to protect my home and finances. I have learned how to analyze a situation so that I will not be totally dependent on a man or anyone to make crucial decisions for me. I even have honed basic home-repair skills and know how to handle a drill, a hammer, and a paintbrush. I have learned how to be a feminine woman, a great mother, and a private woman. I have learned, most of all, how to be caring and loving without allowing others to take advantage of me.

I think we all tried to keep Church Street together at some point and time in our lives, but the drugs and addiction ravaged through all of us in the end, and the only power that was greater than Church Street and the demons that attempted to destroy us all was and is Jesus Christ. It's sad that we lost years of our lives and such a precious treasure in a house built just for us, but it's great that we can share our story today.

Straight from the heart,
Sadie

Divas,

Bernie loved spring. Even until the day she died, she was hoping for the newness that spring would bring. I remember when she was sick she said, "I will feel better when spring comes." Even though her burial date was not spring on the calendar, I remember her gravesite being covered by the sun of spring, which was attempting to peak through, just for her.

Spring was a time when she would plant flowers in the flowerbed in the front of the house. She took pride in planting her flowers, and I took pride in being able to help her to sow the seeds. She planted from the seed, not those pre-grown plants you can

Wrapping It Up

buy these days. Her marigolds, roses, snap dragons and other flowers received her tender loving care from the seed.

I think about the phrase, "Put some spring in your step," and I interpret that to mean, "Pick up the pace—don't let life drag you down or slow down your step." Yes, storms come and storms go, but keep stepping, sisters—put that spring in your step! After all, it was and still is those storms that make the seeds grow into beautiful flowers. Bernie kept spring in her step during her illness and until her death, and so can we! As I mature, I want to surround myself with older, wiser women, so I can learn from them and in turn pass this knowledge to the next generation of women. I want to be able to give back.

Bernie was broken in so many places, but she did the best she could. I don't think about what I could or should have got from her anymore, even though I used to, and it has been a process. Brenda helped me with that after Bernie stole my Sade cassettes and my nice big silver spoon to cook her heroin in and neglected my kids when she was supposed to be babysitting them. I remember the time she babysat them and I came home from work and Naomi was crying, Joshua was digging in the garbage, and Bernie was asleep.

I was so mad, I told Brenda, "She wasn't a good mother, but can't she at least be a grandmother?" Brenda said to me with the softest voice, "Don't be mad at her, Julie." I am so grateful for that, because I received it in my spirit. I now realize Bernie was not capable of babysitting or giving me what I wanted or needed most of that time.

However, even with this understanding and forgiveness, I can't help but go back to the memory of laying my head on her chest when she was on her deathbed in her apartment and crying and telling her that I loved her and I was sad she was in pain and dying. I don't remember her telling me she loved me back, but I do remember her saying, "It's okay, but move over—that hurts."

I was lying on an area that was painful because of the cancer. I remember thinking, "Dang, all I wanted once and for all was some comfort from my mother and she is still not able to give me that." When I think of that now, I think how selfish that was, because she was the one in pain and dying, not me!

Bernie is my strength, an always presence in times of struggle. Her picture is the only one I have on my desk at work and the first one I put up in my new apartment. She reminds me that, no matter what, I am a survivor, a conqueror, and I have strength in the midst of whatever life may throw at me. I am ever grateful to her for passing that down to me and I will love and admire her always!

With love,
Jewels

Hey Divas,

This ongoing communication that keeps us connected and allows us to reflect on the past and stay strong in the present is important to me. The older I get, the more I realize how precious time is. It sounds crazy to me to say I am going to be fifty-nine next year, not to mention that Big Diva turned sixty and has kicked open the door to a new decade of life in numbers, and we hope to be able to follow after her.

On her recent visit with me, about a week after her birthday, my big sister and I talked about life and death. We talked about our mother and her sixty seemingly short years lived on earth. We both confessed to having anxiety about that number, wondering if we would reach it in our life or not. It was not a morbid or sad conversation, but liberating to speak the truth about what was on our minds.

Wrapping It Up

I told her it was just like the thought I had about dying at thirty-eight, the age my father passed away, and I believe that surely would have come to pass had I not gotten sober. I would have killed myself in my addiction or somebody else, or perhaps someone might have killed me, but I do know that death was always over my shoulder. I could feel it every day that I woke up—this is something that I cannot quite put into words. In any case, Big Diva and I ended that brief talk being thankful to God for the life we have and how He has kept us all, and we went on to enjoy sister time, eating, shopping, laughing, and worshipping God together.

September is still a hard month. Though we have the most family birthdays to celebrate and it's a joyous time, it is also the birthday month for our mother, and every year I feel different about it. Sometimes I am so sad I can hardly stand it. I miss her so much it hurts. Over the years I have gone to the Hallmark Shop and looked at cards, and one year I even bought her one. I still have the last birthday cards she received on her sixtieth tucked away in her memory box, but I didn't pull them out this year. I had decided that I was all right in 2013, as sixteen years is a long time and surely grief subsides at some point.

Having Marilyn with me those days, laughing just like Bernie, was so good, and that I believe helped me to fool myself into thinking our mother's death, remembered at her coming birthday, was not going to hurt me the way it used to.

On the day of her birthday, my husband, who loved her deeply, put a bouquet of carnations on the kitchen table, which was an unspoken apology for some of his craziness, and in the middle, he put in a beautiful pink rose, and then left a note saying that that single flower was for our mother. At that moment, all the sadness and anxiety I had been feeling came out, and I had myself a good, long, hard cry at the table, and it felt good. Then I sent y'all the

Diva Five Alive

picture I took on my phone, as I wanted to share that moment with the women who are most important in my life, my sisters, and with the men, also, our brothers. I just felt like I wanted to connect and somehow, I had the sense that our mom was looking over each one of us at that very moment.

I had some different subject matter planned for this letter, but I decided, forget all that, I would take a moment, sit down, and type out my thoughts now, because now is really the only moment I am sure of and I don't want to leave anything important undone. Time and distance may separate us, and I certainly feel isolated and alone not being near any family or friends, but I must continue to make the effort to make time for what matters to me.

I will close with the words that my church elder whom I have adopted as my "elder-dad" says: "We need to live each day as if it were our last." He is going to be eighty-nine years old in December and never misses church or Bible study. I would imagine those words have been his philosophy on life for a long time. I say it often because it's simple and true.

Now, as the new season is upon us, the first day of the tenth month of the year having flown by, I am going to take those words a little more to heart and ask God to help me do that, because we just don't know what day will be the last. As the psalmist wrote, "This is the day the Lord has made and we shall rejoice and be glad in it!" (Psalm 118:24).

Love to my sisters until we speak, write, or text again,

Smooches,

Peace and Love,
Lil Diva

About the Contributors

MARILYN ELIZABETH MCBRIDE (BIG DIVA)

Marilyn was born and raised in Evanston, Illinois. She was raised by our grandparents, Clifton and Sally McBride. At age nineteen, she gave birth to a son, Maurice. When she got heavy into drugs, Maurice went to live with his father and stepmother. Marilyn lived for many years  on the West Side of Chicago. She has been sober for over fifteen years and has worked as a Ryan White case manager, group facilitator, substance abuse case manager, and advocate. She is currently the building manager at her residence for seniors in Kenosha, Wisconsin. Marilyn has been living with HIV for many years and continues to speak to women with the disease, offering strength and hope. She has a wonderful relationship with her son and is a grandmother and great-grandmother.

BRENDA JEAN GIBERT-MILLER (LIL DIVA)

Brenda was born and raised in Evanston, Illinois. Most of her adult life, she lived on the Near North Side of Chicago. She currently resides in Decatur, Illinois.

Brenda began attending First Church of God Christian Life Center in Evanston, Illinois, in March of 1990. It was there that she began her relationship with God and accepted the call to ministry in August of 1991. She was licensed as a minister in 1996 and ordained in 1998. Brenda served as senior associate pastor of First Church from February of 2002 until she moved to Decatur, Illinois, to accept a senior pastor position in April of 2005. Brenda attended The Midwest School of Ministry and Theological Studies on the Church campus in Evanston and received a certificate in Outreach and Evangelism.

To fulfill her desire to help those struggling with alcohol and drug addiction, she completed the Clinical Training Program for Addiction Counselors at Grant Hospital. The program prepared her for the Illinois drug counselor license exam and she maintained her credential requirements for a decade. Brenda earned an Associate Degree in Mental Health from Harold Washington College in Chicago and worked in residential treatment centers for five years before entering full-time ministry.

She has been married to her devoted husband Ken for twenty-six years. She is a stepmother, loving aunt, and spiritual mother to many. Pastor Brenda is fully committed to the ministry of the gospel of Jesus Christ. She knows that her personal testimony is proof that the power of God can change people's lives.

Wrapping It Up

CAROLYN RUTH GIBERT (SADIE AND GRANNY)

Carolyn was born and raised in Evanston, Illinois, and in 1989 relocated to Wisconsin, where she went to college. Carolyn graduated with honors from The Milwaukee Area Technical College with an Associate of Science Degree in Liberal Arts and Science and was the recipient of  the Donna G. Robinson Scholarship. She graduated Magna Cum Laude with a Bachelor of Science in Education from the School of Education at the University of Wisconsin at Milwaukee, where she was the recipient of the Bill and Melinda Gates Scholarship and was a Ronald E. McNair Scholar. She also became a certified English teacher (for grades six through twelve). She received a Master of Science Degree in Administrative Leadership with a focus on Instructional Design from the School of Education at the University of Wisconsin at Milwaukee, where she again graduated with honors and continued to be a recipient of the Bill and Melinda Gates Scholarship.

Carolyn is living with sickle cell anemia and is an advocate for the best treatment for herself and others.

Carolyn is the owner of Nylorack Virtual Enterprises, LLC, a company that provides online virtual instruction for grade school though adult education, with an emphasis on reading comprehension, oral interpretation, writing and editing skills, and teaching online instructional design. She currently resides in Georgia and has one daughter, Jocelyn.

JULIE ANN GIBERT-GRAY (JEWELS)

Julie Ann Gibert-Gray was born and raised in Evanston, Illinois, and spent the majority of her life living in Evanston and on the North Side of Chicago. Julie relocated to Los Angeles, California, in 2010. She is the proud mother of four adult children, Nicole, Lauren, Joshua, and Naomi, and the proud grandmother of two granddaughters, Annmarie and Leila.

Julie obtained a Bachelor of Science Degree in Applied Behavioral Science from National Louis University in Chicago, Illinois, a Master's in Social Work from the University of Illinois at Chicago, Jane Addams School of Social Work, a certificate in School Social Work from Loyola University in Chicago, and a PsyD., with an emphasis in Marriage and Family Therapy from The Chicago School of Professional Psychology.

She has spent the majority of her social services career working at various non-profit agencies as a clinician, supervisor, and administrator. In July of 2017, Julie opened up her own private psychotherapy practice in Torrance, California, where she treats individuals who have experienced trauma, substance abuse, co-dependency, growing up in dysfunctional families, depression, and anxiety. She enjoys working with female survivors of childhood sexual abuse.

Wrapping It Up

EVETTE MARIE GIBERT (MS. EVETTE)

Evette was born and raised in Evanston, Illinois, where she spent the first twenty-six years of her life. After graduating from Evanston Township High School, she landed her first job at an insurance company, where she worked for eleven years. At the age of twenty, Evette gave birth to her daughter, Chanda. She got married in the early eighties and had another daughter, Tiffany, and a son, Paul. She was divorced soon after that. Evette moved around to a couple of different cities and landed back in Chicago, where she currently lives. She has three beautiful grandchildren and one great-grandchild. For the past five years, she has worked as a crewmember at McDonald's and is living life on life's terms! At the time of this book's printing, Evette has since got married! She married Bernard Allen on June 9th, 2018.

Acknowledgements

I give thanks to God, who continues to lead and guide me, even when I am not aware or ask. It is the Spirit of God that has and continues to sustain me, even in my times of fear and uncertainty.

I am thankful for the real Diva, Bernadine Elizabeth McBride-Gibert. Through her struggles and pain, we all learned what real courage looks like.

I am thankful for my Divas—Marilyn, Brenda, Carolyn, and Evette—who willingly agreed to take part in this letter-writing project.

I am also thankful for Melisa Alaba, who coached me through the process of putting this book together and for believing in me. Melisa was a gentle, but persistent guide, who continued to encourage me until the book was done.

I am most thankful for a life that continues to challenge me to do more and to be the best I can be.